ast-into-Present Series

VARFARE

Iichael Palmer

ior History Master,
kmansworth School

B. T. BATSFORD LTD London

First published 1972

ISBN 0 7134 1775 7

Filmset by Keyspools Ltd, Golborne, Lancs.
Printed and bound in Great Britain by
The Anchor Press Ltd, Tiptree, Essex
for the Publishers
B. T. Batsford Ltd, 4 Fitzhardinge Street, London W1

Acknowledgment

The author and the publishers wish to thank the following for permission to reproduce the illustrations in this book: The Duke of Northumberland for fig. 20; the Imperial War Museum for figs. 42, 44, 49, 50, 52, 53, 54 and 58(b); A. W. Kerr for fig. 18; Keystone Press Agency for figs. 48, 55, 58(b), 67 and 68; Mansell Collection for figs. 12, 14 and 29; Mary Evans Picture Library for figs. 11 and 35; Ministry of Public Building and Works for figs. 7 and 21; the Parker Gallery for fig. 32; the Radio Times Hulton Picture Library for figs. 1, 2, 3, 4, 5, 6, 8, 9, 10, 13, 15, 16, 17, 19, 22, 23, 24, 25, 26, 27, 28, 30, 31, 34, 36, 37, 39, 40, 41, 43, 46, 47, 56, 57, 59, 60, 61, 62, 63, 64, 65, 66 and 69.

Contents

The Illustrations

Introduction

Warfare has existed from the very beginning as a basic animal instinct. The first battles would have been between individuals with their bare hands and later with the help of sticks and stones. More elaborate warfare was made possible by the organisation of armies armed with metal weapons and, very early in history, battles were fought between ships on the sea. These wars tended to be limited in their scope and did not involve the majority of the population, who would stay at home farming and keeping house. They might suffer conquest, but even this would not greatly alter their way of life. The scale of warfare increased in the time of Napoleon, when he made the whole male population in France liable for call-up into the army, but its nature was still very similar to what it had always been, confrontations between organised armies and navies. A change in the nature of war occurred in this century, when not only was the whole economy of countries at war geared to war production with women taking the man's place in the factory, but also aircraft carried the war to the civilians at home through aerial bombardment. This was the situation in both the First and Second World Wars. Since then, science has taken control with its invention of various weapons of total destruction, which have given warfare an entirely new potential.

1 Medieval Warfare

Ancient warfare

Soldiers were organised into armies almost as soon as civilised settlements began. One of the earliest Sumerian sculptures from Babylonia, carved around 3000 BC, shows soldiers fighting in close order, wearing helmets and carrying spears and shields. This fighting order developed later in Sumeria into the characteristic organisation of infantry on the battlefield, called the phalanx. Phalanx is a word of Greek origin and describes an army of heavily armed infantry drawn up, in an unbroken line, shoulder to shoulder, with each man holding his long spear in front of him, anchored by his foot and pointing slightly upwards. If it held steady, it had the spiky virtues of a hedgehog in defence and could move forward in perfect order as a formation in attack. It was perfected by the Greeks. The Greek infantry man was called a hoplite and the hoplites who manned the phalanx were equipped with a heavy corselet (body armour) of leather, greaves to defend the shins, an eight-foot pike for thrusting and a two-foot double-edged sword. The hoplites were employed by the Greek city-states and, in the case of Sparta, the whole social structure was geared to war. Their youth began military training at the age of seven and were liable for military service up to the age of sixty.

The army of Alexander the Great, king of Macedonia, was also built round the phalanx of hoplites, supplemented by groups of disciplined light infantry called peltasts. Alexander's phalanx was sixteen ranks deep, divided into tactical masses of 1,024 men abreast and armed with eighteen-foot pikes. Although his Greek Empire in Asia did not long outlast his death in 323 BC, the phalanx remained the basic battle formation of all oriental armies for many years. Discipline and experience were vital in the phalanx, so that often professional soldiers, who gave their services to any king for pay, were employed to give steadiness in the ranks. Such soldiers were called mercenaries.

The chief innovation in ancient warfare was the horse. With the help of this powerful and terrifying animal, the Hyksos, an Asiatic nomadic tribe, temporarily conquered Egypt in 1750 BC. As the saddle, the bridle and the bit were not invented at the time, control was very difficult, but it did make armies very mobile. The Assyrians later terrorised the settlements of the Eastern Mediterranean by their uncouth behaviour and cruel attacks between 850 BC and 650 BC. Assyrian strength lay in their archers and mounted lancers, who fought from horseback without saddles.

The history of Rome is the history of its army and the characteristic army unit was the legion. At first the Roman army was a citizen army, whose main armament was the thrusting spear (hasta) used in the phalanx. This formation

1 A Testudo. This was used by the Roman army to approach a city wall during a siege. The shields were locked together to form a defensive roof against the missiles and thrusting spears of the enemy. Testudo is the Latin for tortoise.

was very suitable while the army was fighting in the neighbourhood of Rome on the plains of Latium, but it became less manageable once they advanced into the hills of Italy. Thereafter the legions broke up into small groups (maniples) of 120 and the throwing spear (pilum) replaced the hasta. The pilum, a small shield, a helmet with cheek pieces to defend the face and a short stabbing sword became the standard equipment of the Roman legionary from then on.

The legions that attacked Britain in AD 43 were 5–6,000 strong, divided into 10 cohorts and 60 centuries. Members of the legions had to be Roman citizens and had to serve for a twenty year engagement. The legionary was extremely mobile. He carried 40 pounds of equipment, including three days' rations, a saw, an axe, an entrenching tool, a wicker basket for carrying earth and a mess tin. Moreover, the fine Roman roads enabled legions to march quickly from one point to another on good hard surfaces. Once they conquered a country like Britain, they settled down in permanent camps in garrison towns like Caerleon, Chester and York or next to permanent defences like Hadrian's Wall. They were supported by regiments of cavalry in battle and were helped in their more onerous duties by auxiliary regiments, recruited from the barbarian tribes that

2 Roman Centurions: members of the Praetorian Cohorts formed by Emperor Augustus to serve as the Imperial bodyguard. They were volunteers and enjoyed better pay and shorter service than the regular army. They were housed in fortified barracks on the edge of the city of Rome. A centurion commanded a troop of one hundred men.

they conquered. It was partly the dilution of the Roman army by barbarians in this way and partly the novel use of cavalry in attack by the Goths at the battle of Adrianople in AD 378, that checked the long domination of the Roman army over Europe. In the fourth century AD, the saddle, the stirrup, the horseshoe and a heavier breed of warhorse appeared in the Ukraine and on the Persian plateau and these were to give predominance to the cavalry for the next thousand years.

The Fyrd and the Feudal Army

The Roman legions left Britain in AD 410 to defend Rome from barbarian attack and very soon the Angles and Saxons began to settle in what can now be called England. The Celts, who lived in Wales and Cornwall, did not present a very great threat, so the Anglo-Saxons retained their original German people's army or militia for military purposes, while their continental equivalents were adopting a feudal organisation under which the king's vassals were expected to bring armed cavalry and footsoldiers to the king's army as part of their expression of allegiance. The coastal raids and eventual invasion of the Vikings forced the Anglo-Saxon kings to pay more attention to military preparation. The Vikings were well armed, with battle axes and double-edged swords and defended their bodies with mail byrnies (mail shirts) and steel caps. They were also very experienced members of war bands and found themselves pitted against Anglo-Saxon farmers. Alfred the Great, King of Wessex, was forced to produce heavy armed infantrymen quickly. He therefore called up his militia, which was known as the fyrd. It was divided into two halves so that only half the farmers would be taken from the land at any time. The more important freeholders were made thanes and were expected to supply themselves with heavy armament, though not with horses.

Rapid adaptation enabled Alfred to defeat Guthrum at the battle of Edington (AD 878) and to force the Vikings to remain on the east side of Watling Street in the area known as the Danelaw. When the country became united again under King Canute, a new military element was introduced in the form of the housecarls. These were a professional body of household troops, armed with the long Danish battle-axe, which could only be wielded on foot. The fyrd and the housecarls were the basis of Harold's army at the battle of Hastings. The army had horses, but before battle they dismounted and formed a compact mass. Harold's army, blocking William the Conqueror's path to London on Senlac Hill on the 14 October, 1066, would have been unconquered had some of the fyrd not left their positions in pursuit of the Norman horsemen, who feigned flight. Once the line was broken, volleys of arrows followed by cavalry attacks eventually gave William victory.

William, who was used to continental war organisation, introduced the system of military feudalism into England, by which his vassals were to supply him with his knights and footsoldiers, in return for their land. The system never

3 The Bayeux Tapestry. This famous tapestry illustrates the Norman Conquest of England in 1066. This section shows the death of Harold and is the origin of the story that Harold was killed by an arrow which struck him in the eye. Notice the chain mail suits (byrnies) in the central picture and the method of removing them on the frieze. The soldiers wore conical helmets with nasals to defend the nose. They fought with double-edged swords, shields and battle-axes.

proved suitable for English needs, especially as feudal service was limited to 40 days each year. Armies were needed to fight on the continent in Normandy and later in Gascony and Aquitaine, where much longer service was necessary. There was also no great inducement for substantial landowners to become knights. They were not an exclusive warrior class nor did they enjoy any tax exemption; in fact, the winning of a knight's fief (feudal estate) lay open to all freemen. The emphasis on chivalry and individual gallantry was helped by the introduction of tournaments by King Stephen. At these events, knights in their armour would ride at each other with lances at the horizontal and attempt to unseat their opponent. Yet, there still seems to have been a steady decline in the number of knights.

Henry II (1154–77) began to change the system by allowing knights to pay a tax called scutage instead of serving in the army, or alternatively he asked three knights to furnish and equip one of their number. He also re-established the fyrd by his Assize of Arms (1181). These reforms were elaborated by subsequent kings especially by Edward I (1272–1307). He superseded the summoning of the feudal army by issuing commissions to one or two leading men of the county to muster and array the military forces. Such commissions were issued right up to the time of Charles I. He also cherished the fyrd by clarifying the Assize of Arms in the Statute of Winchester (1285). He specified what weapons and equipment each class of people should possess, from the rich freeman, who was to have an iron hauberk (a complete set of mail), a sword, a knife and a horse, to the lowest peasant, who was to have a bow and arrows. These archers were to have no armour and were to prove astonishingly successful as light infantry in the next 100 years.

The Archer

The period from 1338 to 1453 was a period of endemic war with France known as the Hundred Years' War. During this time the army to fight on the continent was formed by making contracts with men of position to serve the king with a force of fixed strength during a fixed term and at a fixed rate of pay. The soldiers were rather like mercenaries except that they were all fellow countrymen. In esteem, the mounted men at arms, who under the Statute of Winchester included the richest freemen, were the most important arm. The man at arms would normally have three horses. The best horse was called a dextrarius, because it was led by the shield bearer on the right-hand side (dexter means 'right' in Latin), but he would also have a palfrey for normal riding and a packhorse for baggage. The paraphernalia of war was considerable, especially as it became usual to cover the war-horse with armour after 1300. In France, the feudal army still existed. It was very difficult to command as it was full of noblemen and knights, trained to think of themselves as warriors, who fought as individuals

4 Left: Twelfth century knight of the Crusades. The body armour is still chain-mail with a white tunic to deflect the heat of the sun. The horse has similar armour, including an elaborate helmet.

5 Right: Fourteenth century knight with the heavier and more elaborate plate mail that became the normal armour for men-at-arms in the 100 Years War. The plate is carefully hinged to allow movement and angled to deflect the lance thrusts of the enemy.

6 Medieval siege. The soldiers are mainly armed with long bows but there are two crossbowmen, one on each side. In the bottom right hand corner is a large siege gun capable of blasting a breach in a city wall.

rather than as part of an army. The only way to use the cavalry was in large masses, advancing at the trot, knee to knee, so that the enemy would be pushed aside by the weight of the attack.

The English archers were sometimes mounted, but always fought on foot. Their bows, made of yew, were six feet high and fired arrows a yard long, fitted with barbs and points of iron and fledged with goose or peacock feathers. They were trained from childhood to use a bow so that they could develop the strength to pull the bow string to their ear and the accuracy to kill at 100 yards. The falling arrow could carry with ease for 240 yards and was capable of searching out the chinks and weaknesses in armour. Their equivalent on the French side was the Genoese crossbowman, who had an equally deadly weapon, but could only discharge three bolts in the time that it took for the longbowman to fire twelve arrows. The longbowmen could also stand in much closer order behind their common palisade of stakes. The stakes were pointed and were directed towards the enemy so that they would impale enemy horses that charged at the bowmen.

The archers met with their first successes during Edward I's wars with Wales and Scotland. They opened up a way into the serried ranks of Scottish pikemen

at Falkirk in 1298, though Edward II's defeat by the Scots at Bannockburn in 1314 showed that neither cavalry nor archers on their own could defeat pikemen; it had to be a skilful co-ordination of the two weapons to bring victory. In the three key battles of the Hundred Years' War at Crecy (1346), Poitiers (1356) and Agincourt (1415), the English gained the victory, although on each occasion they were outnumbered, because the French chose to attack the English in a good defensive position. When Edward III took his expedition to France in 1346, he set out with 4,000 men-at-arms, 10,000 archers and 6,000 Welsh spearmen; he was matched by a French army of 20,000 men-at-arms and 15,000 infantry. The English men-at-arms fought on foot and victory was gained as a result of their steadiness and the disruption caused by the English archers. At Crecy the French lost at least 10,000 killed against English casualties of two knights, an esquire and perhaps 100 other ranks.

The French concluded that the victory at Crecy must have been won by the well-born men-at-arms and therefore tried to compensate for their deficiencies at Crecy, by fighting on foot at Poitiers in 1356. Once again the French were demoralised by the shower of arrows that rained on them before they had reached the English line. For some time after their defeat at Poitiers, the French nobles returned to their castles and allowed the English armies to march through the length and breadth of the land unmolested, until they were exhausted by food shortages and disease. When the nobility of France once more took the field against Henry V at Agincourt in 1415, nothing had been learnt. A great army of French knights defeated themselves in the face of a very small English army of 6,000, by marching on foot into the attack across ploughed fields, sodden with a week of rain. Henry's army was also dismounted and watched the French army wallow in confusion, when the arrows began to fall. Henry awaited his chance and then ordered the archers to put aside their bows and fall to with axe and sword. The low-born bowmen 'beat upon the armour with mallets as though they were smiths hammering upon anvils', and in the face of this ferocity the third French line melted away without making a charge. Once Joan of Arc raised French morale and Dunois and La Hire adopted sounder tactics, it was soon shown that the superiority of the bow depended on the ability of the bowmen to keep the enemy at a distance. By 1453, the English presence on the continent was confined to Calais and English influence on European warfare came to an end.

7 Beaumaris Castle is the best example of a concentric castle with a ring of fortifications. The main living rooms would be in the far gate house with flags flying from the turrets. Each turret was capable of being defended as an individual fortress. The second picture shows Beaumaris Castle as it is today.

Siege Warfare

One of the most striking features of medieval warfare was the importance of fortified places. If battles were few, sieges were numerous and very long. The castle was an integral part of feudal organisation. The motte and bailey castles built in William the Conqueror's reign, provided a keep on top of a mound (motte) for a military garrison and a defended courtyard (bailey) for the villagers and their cattle. In the reign of Edward I, more elaborate castles like those in North Wales were built. The lay-out of these castles was adapted to the site, but the authentic plan of an Edwardian castle is to be seen at Beaumaris, which is built on a flat site on Anglesey. There is no keep, but the two circular walls have towers at intervals, which can be defended as if they were keeps and the gateways are heavily fortified and became the main living quarters in the castle.

The castle walls were phenomenally thick and were often further defended against mining by a moat. If the enemy could fill the moat and work at the base of the wall, it was difficult for the castle garrison to stop them without exposing themselves to fire. This weakness in castles was overcome by building flanking towers from which the base of the wall could be seen without difficulty and by the use of machicolation, which is a projection of the top of the wall, so that the defenders can look through a hole onto the bottom of the outer wall.

The safety of the nobleman in his castle made it possible for nobles to defy the king and the danger from overmighty subjects was increased by the tradition which allowed them to enlist private armies, which were then hired to the king. The end of the Hundred Years' War in France was followed by a period of Civil War in England known as the Wars of the Roses. In the background of the feudal disorder, was a struggle for control of the throne between the House of Lancaster and the House of York. One of the factors which made it possible for kings to control their powerful subjects was the introduction of gunpowder into Europe. Artillery in battle had been used to create terror rather than win battles since Crecy, but as a siege weapon it was decisive. In 1453, the Turks captured Constantinople after only six weeks by battering the walls down with artillery and thereafter thick walls ceased to be a sure defence. One of the symbols of Henry VII's power after he had defeated the Yorkists at Bosworth in 1485 was a train of artillery, but by then, castle architecture was already beginning to reflect military change by incorporating thinner walls and windows. The use of gunpowder in guns and cannons was also gradually to change the art of warfare.

FURTHER READING

Lord Montgomery of Alamein, *A History of Warfare* (Collins).
R. E. Oakeshott, *A Knight and his Armour* (Lutterworth).
Sir Charles Oman, *A History of the Art of War in the Middle Ages* (Lutterworth).
R. R. Sellman, *Mediaeval English Warfare* (Methuen).

2 The Age of the Militia

The period from 1485 to 1660 can be called the Age of the Militia, because the monarchs gradually came to rely on home recruitment for their foreign wars and depended almost entirely on the shire levies for the subjugation of rebellions that occurred in 1536, 1549 and 1569. The Civil Wars too can be seen as attempts by the two sides to control the system of shire recruitment, the King by Commissions of Array and the Parliament by a Militia Ordinance. There was little in the way of a regular army. Henry VIII's 'gentlemen pensioners' and his yeomen of the guard amounted to no more than a personal bodyguard. Henry was in the habit of taking foreign mercenary troops into his pay, but his example was not copied by Elizabeth, probably for financial reasons. Only in the battles with the Scots at Flodden (1513) and Solway Moss (1542) did he rely wholly on the northern shire levies. He hired 500 'Almaynes' (Germans) for his first expedition to Bayonne in 1512, and 5,000 for his campaign against Boulogne in 1544. Many of these Germans were pikemen.

The Pike and Musket

The great advantage of the pike was that it was a cheap reliable weapon. Its virtues were rediscovered by the Swiss in the fourteenth and fifteenth centuries. They used the pikemen as a fast, mobile attacking infantry in the Swiss wars with the Hapsburgs and the Burgundians. They were too poor to be able to afford the accoutrements of war and wore the minimum of armour. It was lightness coupled with discipline that enabled them to move rapidly into the attack with their eighteen-foot pike carried shoulder high and pointed slightly downwards into the bodies of the enemy. Like the English bowmen, they revealed the weaknesses of the feudal cavalry and showed that a peasant army could defeat a noble one. The services of the Swiss were much in demand in the Italian wars which started in 1494, but in Italy their success in attack was less, when faced with equally professional armies. Nevertheless, the pike remained a favoured weapon until it was superseded by the bayonet at the end of the seventeenth century.

The traditional English equivalent of the pike was the bill, which was a broad curved blade mounted at the end of a seven foot shaft, with a point and hook added. Together with the bow it was the most common weapon in England. The battles of the Wars of the Roses were mainly fought by armies composed of masses of billmen, flanked by wings of archers. In England, the pike gradually replaced the bill and its close equivalent the halberd. It was used as a weapon of defence and was mainly used to cover and defend the musketeers. The most readily available pikemen in the early sixteenth century were the German

8 Pike drill. Elaborate movements were needed to manipulate the eighteen-foot long pike especially when the pikemen were standing in close order. The pikeman wore half armour and a metal helmet.

landsnechts, who had proved themselves to be a match for the Swiss. At Flodden, the Scots had studied the methods of the landsnechts and had imported enormous quantities of long pikes for the coming battle, but on this occasion the English bill and bow prevailed. Pikes were no use on their own and by 1544, Henry VIII was beginning to understand their use in conjunction with arquebusiers. After her accession, Elizabeth also armed the trained bands with light muskets (calivers) and pikes.

Around 1480, the invention of an S-shaped holder for the slow match and of a trigger which released the match into the flashpan, made the match-lock arquebus a potential war weapon. At first, they were heavy and cumbersome, but around the middle of the sixteenth century, muskets about three feet long, firing one leaden shot every two minutes were capable of being fired without the use of a rest. Before this, muskets had been so long and heavy that they could only be fired with the muzzle of the weapon resting on a forked stand. Although the shorter musket enabled musketeers to do without a rest the musketeer was greatly encumbered by the equipment necessary to effect a successful shot. Strung across his chest he wore a dozen small containers each with a charge of powder. He also had a small horn containing fire powder for priming and a bag full of bullets. Each shot had to be muzzle loaded and the weapons were extremely inaccurate. Nevertheless, everyone wanted to be a musketeer. As de Fourqueraux said, 'I know not whether it be to take more wages, or to be lighter laden, or to be further off'.

9 The Musketeer was a seventeenth century soldier, yet he still carries a stand on which he could rest the long heavy musket when firing. He has a shoulder strap from which hangs his bullet bag and a festoon of small containers each containing powder for one shot. The horn of priming powder hangs from his waist belt. He has a lighted double ended match cord between his fingers.

The Tudor Army

In 1558, Mary Tudor passed an Act concerning the militia which superseded the Statute of Winchester. There were to be ten class groups between those who earned £1,000 a year and those who earned between £5 and £10 a year. The richest had to supply sixteen horses, sixty suits of light armour, forty pikes, twenty bills or halberds, twenty arquebuses, fifty iron helmets and thirty long bows with arrows, while the poorest were required to keep a coat of plated armour, a bill or a halberd, a long bow with arrows and an iron helmet. In this way there should have been a potential army of around 300,000 men, as all able-bodied men between the ages of sixteen and sixty were liable for service with the militia. In reality, only a certain proportion of each county was kept in training, at most 12 per cent of those eligible; these were known as the trained bands. The most famous trained bands were those of London, which showed themselves in good shape during the invasion crisis of 1539, when Emperor Charles V threatened to invade. Fifteen thousand men, all able-bodied and properly equipped, paraded past the king, all dressed in white and led by the artillery. These trained bands were predominantly a home defence force and other methods had to be used to recruit an army for a foreign expedition.

10 Halberd drill. The halberd (or halbert) was an elaboration of the bill. It incorporates a stabbing spear, a chopper and a hooking knife. This was the standard weapon for a common soldier in the sixteenth century.

Elizabeth was always very short of money and had to depend too greatly on the free services of her subjects for army recruitment. The burden of recruitment was placed on the Lords Lieutenant in the county and they shared the task with the Justices of the Peace as commissioners of musters. The easiest way for them was to fill the army with riff-raff and to give the positions of responsibility and reward to their friends. Barnaby Rich in 1578 wrote that 'In London, when they set forth soldiers, either they scour their prisons of thieves or their streets of vagabonds, for he that is bound to find a man will seek such a one that is better lost than found.' A speaker in the House of Commons said in 1601, that 'the justice of the peace is a living creature, yet for half a dozen chickens will dispense with a whole dozen of penal statutes. . . . If a warrant come from the Lords of the Council to levy 100 men, he will levy 200 and what with chopping in and choosing out he'll gain a 100 pounds by the bargain.'

The most corrupt officials, however, were the captains, who took charge of the companies overseas and were responsible for every aspect of the soldiers' life, his pay, his uniform and his weapons. The company was between 100 and 200 strong and there would be ten of them to a regiment. All the money and equipment for the soldiers passed through the hands of the captain and there were many ways by which he could enrich himself. They were capable of sending off their men on dangerous missions, knowing that every man killed would be an extra 'dead pay' for their own pocket. They were also not beneath selling off the uniforms and weapons privately and ignoring their own troops' needs. The captains' malpractices should have been discovered at the monthly musters that were held on active service. If all muster-masters had been as efficient as Thomas Digges, they would have been. It was often possible, however, for captains to bribe the muster officials and thus cover up the gaps in their companies and the missing weapons and uniforms.

The soldiers' pay was 8d a day, but on service they only received enough to provide their food, clothing and gunpowder, the balance being paid every six months. They had to buy their food from victuallers and their uniform and powder from the captain, both of whom were liable to cheat them. The normal diet was loaf bread or biscuit, butter, cheese and beer; the daily beer ration was one gallon. Uniforms varied from county to county and depended on the whims of the lord lieutenant, but they were often red in colour. By 1589 the ideal company weapons were said to be sixty firearms, thirty pikes and ten halberds or bills. The heavily armed cavalry had virtually disappeared and even the demi-lances, a medium heavy cavalry, were diminishing in number. Mobility was now supplied by the light cavalry, who were to become an important part of the army for the next 300 years.

11 The Militia. Falstaff examining his recruits. Falstaff was an army captain, immortalised in William Shakespeare's two plays on Henry IV. He had the help of the magistrates in choosing recruits from the militia for overseas service. Some were willing to bribe the captain to be overlooked, but ragged Thomas Wart near the fire was recruited.

Foreign War

English armies were drawn onto the continent quite frequently in the sixteenth century. Until the loss of Calais in 1558, England had a permanent bridgehead, expensively maintained by a garrison of bowmen, billmen and gunners. The memory of continental Empire and of England's claim to the French throne died hard and war was normally waged with France until mid-century; thereafter the main threat was felt to be the presence of a Spanish army in the Netherlands, which was too near to England for comfort. France had a long-standing alliance with Scotland, so that whenever war broke out with France, there was danger of a Scots invasion too. Campaigns in France were usually confined to the coastal regions and success was counted in successful sieges. Thérouanne and Tournai surrendered in 1513, when Henry VIII had twelve enormous pieces of artillery called the Twelve Apostles, and Boulogne in 1544. As far as pitch battles were concerned, the English had a victory in the battle of the Spurs (1513), named after the panic flight of the French, and a victory at St Quentin (1557) helped by our Spanish allies, who denuded the Calais garrison of troops and laid it open to French conquest in 1558.

Elizabeth was persuaded by the suffering of her troops from plague at Le Havre in 1563, by the impossibility of sending adequate replacements for the dead and by the perfidy of the French protestants, that a positive foreign policy to regain Calais was beyond her means. She limited her continental involvement to the defence of what she considered were Britain's vital interests. This was that the Channel and North Sea ports from which England could be invaded should not fall into the hands of Spain. She declared war on Spain in 1585 and sent an army of 6,000 across to the Netherlands. Of these 6,000, 4,500 were always to garrison the North Sea ports, especially the deep water port at Flushing. After 1588, she sent a number of expeditions to Brittany to make sure that Brest would not fall into Spanish hands as a result of Spanish intervention in the French Religious Wars. As another method of guaranteeing the naval supremacy that was displayed in the defeat of the Armada (1588), she sent amphibious expeditions, often with large numbers of soldiers, to attack Spanish ships in their ports in 1587, 1589 and 1595.

Elizabeth had always fought her wars on the cheap, but she made very intelligent use of her limited resources. James I and Charles I experienced the same financial embarrassment as the value of royal revenue continued to decline as prices rose, but they made disastrous use of their scanty means between 1624 and 1629. James had sensibly kept peace with Spain as long as he was able, but before he died war was declared on Spain and his successor soon found himself involved in war with France as well. The regular dismal failure of continental expeditions in these years, due to poor recruits, poor leadership and inadequate supplies discredited Stuart monarchy itself. When the Scots threatened to invade in 1639 and actually invaded in 1640 in the Bishops' Wars, the militia that was mustered from both the northern and the southern counties

12 Roundhead soldiers. This picture shows the different weapons and uniforms of soldiers in the New Model Army. The pikeman and the halberdier with a two-pronged halberd wear half-armour, while the musketeer has none at all. All soldiers carry a sword.

proved entirely unfit for the task of withstanding a Scottish army pledged to resist Archbishop Laud's religious policy. Charles I had no choice but to make an ignominious treaty at Ripon (1640) which left the Scots in occupation of the northern counties. This early part of the seventeenth century marks the lowest point in English military history.

The New Model Army

There was a great incentive to develop efficient armies when the quarrel between King and Parliament over the control of government degenerated into war in 1642. Each side tried to mobilise the militia for its own cause; but it soon became clear that such forces were too local in their allegiance and temporary in their service to be suitable for long campaigns. The king's army had a distinct cavalry advantage at first with its higher proportion of landed gentry in its ranks. Prince

13 Cromwell at Marston Moor, 1644. In this battle the Scots helped Parliament to inflict a serious defeat on the Royalists which gave Parliament control of the North. The battle was a personal triumph for Oliver Cromwell, whose Eastern Association cavalry defeated the royalist Cavalry under Prince Rupert and then helped to defeat the royalist infantry in the centre.

14 The Battle of Naseby, 1645. Cromwell's army defended Naseby and held the high ground. The King moved towards him from the direction of Leicester. The cavalry of both armies defended the flanks of the infantry in the centre. The pikemen are seen holding their pikes aloft and are in a position to defend the artillerymen and musketeers. Notice the 'forlorn hope', a group of musketeers sent in front to open the battle from close quarters.

Rupert, the royalist cavalry commander, used the tactics developed by Gustavus Adolphus of Sweden in Germany based on the charge with sword in hand and the use of pistols in the ensuing mêlée. These tactics were successful from a cavalry point of view at Edgehill and Marston Moor, but its fatal weakness was that control of the cavalry was lost and it proved impossible to regroup them for a flank attack on the enemy infantry.

Cromwell as an opponent understood the lesson of Rupert's mistakes and recruited a regiment of cavalry for the Parliament that was eventually to win the cavalry battle and remain under discipline to defeat the opposing infantry. Cromwell was highly selective in his recruitment and taught his troops to advance at the trot knee to knee. Their main weapon was the pair of pistols, which they fired only when they came close to the enemy. They would then use their sword for the main battle, which they won by steady pressure rather than by the shock of a charge. Cromwell's first great victory using these methods was at Marston Moor, where he proved much more successful than Prince Rupert. He said of his victory:

We never charged but we routed the enemy. The left wing which I commanded, being our own horse, saving a few Scots in our rear, beat all the Prince's horse. God made them stubble to our swords.

Before the battle of Naseby 1645, Cromwell's cavalrymen, who had earned the name 'The Ironsides', were amalgamated into the New Model Army. This army was freed of the former noble leadership and was completely professional with promotion only on merit. It was clothed in a uniform tunic of red, the colour adopted as the colour of the infantryman's coat until the end of the nineteenth century.

The infantry in the New Model Army, which outnumbered the cavalry by two to one, was made up of musketeers and pikemen. There were now many more musketeers than pikemen even though their weapon was still very difficult to load. The musketeers formed up in files six deep defended by the pikemen. They might open the battle with a simultaneous discharge called a salvee, but thereafter they would fire in turn and then retire to the rear to recharge. Most muskets still used the matchlock principle, but wheel-lock and flint-lock pistols were usual as the cavalrymen could not ride into battle with matches smouldering. Armour was only worn by the pikemen, who took the brunt of the enemy attack at the end of their sixteen foot pikes. It was the weight of their clothing that made them very poor marchers. Each regiment had two pieces of artillery of the smaller kind called sakers, minions and drakes, which could fire fifteen or so shots an hour. There was also a hybrid regiment of dragoons, who were infantrymen mounted on inferior horses, used for vanguard and rearguard duties such as defending bridges.

This army became one of the most efficient in Europe as the result of its religious discipline and its efficient fighting qualities. Not only did it play an important

15 Oliver Cromwell 1599–1658, a copy of a famous portrait by Peter Lely, painted in 1653. Cromwell is said to have told the artist, 'Paint me, warts and all.' In 1653 Cromwell's power as army leader brought him the title of Protector of England, Scotland and Ireland.

part in Parliament's victory in the Civil Wars in England, but it also subdued Ireland and Scotland and gained an impressive victory on the continent at Dunkirk in 1658. For ten years after the Civil Wars ended, the Army remained under arms and became gradually more and more unpopular. Only very heavy taxation made its existence possible and at one stage the country was placed under direct military rule. For this reason foreigners were much more impressed by England's Army than Englishmen. A royalist in exile on the continent called Edward Hyde, later Lord Clarendon said, 'Cromwell's greatness at home was a mere shadow of his greatness abroad.' The effect of the Army on Englishmen was to persuade them that they never wanted to experience a standing army again.

FURTHER READING

A. Burns and P. Young, *The Great Civil War* (Eyre and Spottiswoode).
S. E. Ellacott, *Guns* (Methuen).
C. H. Firth, *Cromwell's Army* (Methuen).
H. Hansen, *The Civil War* (New English Library).
Sir Charles Oman, *A History of the Art of War in the Sixteenth Century* (Methuen).
R. R. Sellman, *Civil War and Commonwealth* (Methuen).
N. Wymer, *Soldiers and Sailors* (Oxford).

3 Marlborough to Wellington

Standing armies

The military prowess of the New Model Army was not completely lost at the restoration of Charles II in 1660, for the decision was taken to retain a few regiments for the maintenance of order. Some of these regiments, the Life Guards for instance, were raised from among royalist supporters, but the Coldstream Guards and the Royal Horse Guards were recruited from the New Model Army. The history of the regular army starts from 1660 and its existence raised a constitutional problem. For the next century there was continual concern that a standing army under royal control could become an instrument of despotism and there was concrete evidence of this in the reign of James II when the army on Hounslow Heath threatened to be the weapon for a Catholic counter-revolution. When James II was forced to abdicate in 1688, Acts were passed limiting the king's control over finance and releasing the soldiers from military discipline if the king tried to rule without parliament. It was clearly stated that:

> The raising of a standing army within the United Kingdom in time of peace, unless it be with the consent of Parliament, is against the law.

Yet even so there was still concern.

Opponents of royal power preferred the militia, which had the characteristics of a people's army. The militia had a very checkered existence until 1757, when a Militia Act breathed some new life into it. It could hardly be relied on to cope with the Jacobite invasions of 1715 and 1745 when the descendants of James II attempted to claim back the throne. In 1745 the Duke of Cumberland had to bring over mercenary soldiers from Hanover and Hesse, who were often employed to increase the numbers in the British army in time of war. There were therefore both political and military motives in the attempt to revive the militia in 1757 by rendering all males of military age liable to three years' militia service. In fact only a small number were chosen by ballot and it was quite easy to pay someone to be a substitute.

There was some pride in the militia during the Seven Years' War, when invasion was threatened in 1759. A patriotic ballad ran:

> We ask not assistance of Hesse and Hanover,
> Nor need we to fetch our own Englishmen;
> And why should we send for our neighbours the Dutch
> When as many Dutch herrings would serve us as much?
> All over the land they'll find such a stand,
> From our English Militia Men ready at hand.

By the end of the century, however, the justification of the militia as a means of limiting the crown's power had subsided, and during the Napoleonic Wars it became little more than a source of recruits for the fighting army. When peace was made with France in 1815 it was abolished.

Marlborough

Louis XIV's France was the great military power in the latter half of the seventeenth century. She had great military commanders like Condé and Turenne, outstanding military organisers like Louvois and masters of siege and fortification like Vauban. Her field armies were so large that only a coalition of many states could field an army of the same size. Great Britain became deeply involved in the wars against France when the ruler of Holland was invited to take the throne of England as William III in 1688. British troops were fighting in the Netherlands from 1689 onwards, but it was not until 1701 that a leader of genius was placed in charge. This commander was John Churchill, Earl of Marlborough. His task was made much more difficult by the Dutch civilian government, which insisted that he should only use his army in a defensive capacity and it attached field deputies to Marlborough's army to see that he attempted nothing without their permission.

War had tended to become very defensive at this time. Vauban had ringed France with a series of impregnable fortifications, built up on geometrical patterns so that the defence always had an easy killing ground in front of them. In attack, the French armies had become used to long theatrical sieges, which

16 John Churchill, first Duke of Marlborough 1650–1722. The Duke is seen wearing armour, but this was only ceremonial. Cavalry men had not been wearing armour in battle for over a century. The Duke is also carrying his Marshal's baton, the symbol of his rank.

17 The Battle of Blenheim 1704. The picture shows the break through of Marlborough's army and in the distance the French army can be seen attempting flight across the River Danube, which is one hundred yards wide at that point. The French right wing was bottled up in the village of Blenheim.

had a predictable outcome of surrender as Vauban had also mastered the art of approach and siege. Despite all this, Marlborough adopted offensive strategies that enabled him to meet the French army in the open and to win four outstanding victories at Blenheim (1704), Ramillies (1706), Oudenarde (1708) and Malplaquet (1709).

Marlborough was a great organiser, able to cope with the details of supply and always conscious of his soldiers' comfort. This was illustrated by his army's march from the Netherlands to Bavaria in 1704 to stop the French army's advance on Vienna, the capital of Britain's ally, Austria. On this march, 250 miles were covered in under six weeks, at a daily rate of fourteen miles, which was always completed in the cool of the day. Heavy stores and artillery were shipped by river where possible. The result was that at the end of the march the army had achieved surprise and was able to bring the Franco-Bavarian army to battle at Blenheim on the River Danube. Here Marlborough won the day by exploiting a bridge across the River Nebel, a tributary of the Danube, which the French general, Tallard, had left undefended. He was able to concentrate his forces on the French centre at a point where there was a weakness between the French army on the right and the Bavarian army on the left. Marlborough broke through and pinned Tallard's army against the River Danube, where many French soldiers surrendered or drowned in their attempt to escape. This was the first defeat that Louis XIV's army had suffered and for the rest of the war that continued until the Treaty of Utrecht (1713), Louis was thrown onto the defensive.

On the battlefield, Marlborough was able to keep control of his forces even when they were sent into battle in a hurry, as was the case at Oudenarde. He was also able to concentrate his forces at the enemy's point of weakness in such a way as to effect surprise. The break through from such a concentration was in the centre at Blenheim, on the left flank at Ramillies, while at Oudenarde Marlborough managed to outflank the French on the left completely. He achieved all this with an international army whose management demanded all the skills and patience of a seasoned diplomat.

Marlborough was relieved of his command for political reasons in 1711 before the war ended, but already he had been given the manor of Woodstock by the grateful Queen Anne and there he built a great country house, Blenheim, to celebrate his victory.

Military changes

France remained the national enemy for the rest of the eighteenth century and Great Britain became involved in war with France during the following years:

War in Holland against France	1689–1697
War of Spanish Succession – Marlborough's War	1701–1713
War of Austrian Succession	1740–1748
Seven Years' War	1756–1763
War of American Independence	1776–1783
Revolutionary War	1793–1802
Napoleonic War	1803–1815

There were plenty of opportunities for improving the army which reached a size of over 60,000 in the Seven Years' War and the Napoleonic Wars.

By the end of the seventeenth century the flintlock or fusil was in general use and enabled the musketeers to fire a little more quickly. Instead of the old order of six ranks, four, three or even two were felt to be adequate. Pikemen had been made obsolete by the introduction of the socket bayonet, a French invention, in 1693. The first bayonets blocked the muzzle of the musket and proved too difficult to fix in the heat of battle, but the socket bayonet could be fixed before the battle started without hindering the musket's fire. It enabled the musketeer to fight successfully either at long range or at close quarters and the pike was therefore no longer necessary.

Marlborough's cavalrymen were lightly armoured and mobile with just a breastplate. They charged with the sword, which was accepted as the gentleman's main weapon in the eighteenth century. The dragoons were more likely to use

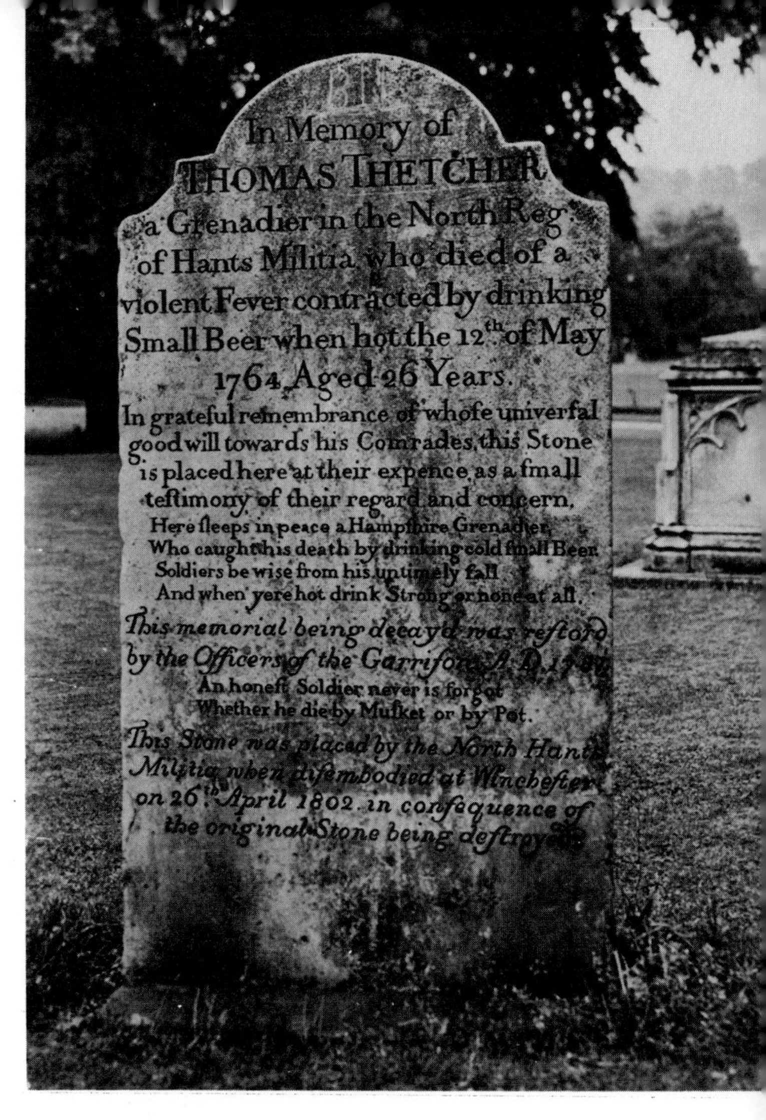

18 This tombstone tells the touching story of a Hampshire militiaman.

carbines or pistols when they began to fight on horse-back instead of dismounting to fight as infantry. Very lightly armed dragoons attached to each regiment became known as hussars, after the Hungarian light cavalry.

The artillery still had no official standing in Marlborough's day and it was not until 1716 that permanent artillery companies were formed at his suggestion. By 1727 there were four such companies and they were formed into the Royal Regiment of Artillery. Another branch of the army that emerged was engineering. Sappers had been used for some time for undermining the walls in sieges, but they gained no separate recognition. The first engineers were an entirely officer corps, trained in the School of Military Engineering that was founded in 1741.

Although soldiers enlisted for life as volunteers, they were attracted by money bounties rather than by the conditions of service. Their pay was still subject to many deductions and there were intentionally very few barracks where they could live in peace time. They were, however, held in some respect when they were billeted out in the houses of private citizens. As Samuel Johnson said,

'When a common soldier is civil in his quarters, his red coat procures him a degree of respect.'

Colonial Wars

Britain never enjoyed the same success in the wars against France and her allies on the continent in the middle part of the eighteenth century as Marlborough had done. In the Seven Years' War, the British government was prepared to allow Frederick the Great of Prussia to bear the main brunt of French, Austrian and Russian attacks, while British troops laid the basis of a colonial Empire at the expense of France and subsequently Spain. A similar policy was followed during the Revolutionary and Napoleonic Wars, now at the expense of French, Dutch and Spanish possessions.

Colonies were valued not so much for their size as for their commodities. The most highly prized were the sugar islands in the Caribbean and the Slave bases on the West African coast. Dramatic military progress was, however, made in America, which was a major colony of settlement, and India, which was an important source of oriental products and spices.

The French had settled the line of the River St Lawrence in Canada and had

19 The capture of Quebec in 1759 was one of the great British victories over the French in the colonies during the Seven Years' War. The landing of the British army on the cliff face of the Heights of Abraham during the night and the battle on the fields above was the achievement of Major-General Wolfe, who lost his life in the ensuing victory.

a series of forts along the River Ohio and the River Mississippi, which acted as a barrier against the potential expansion of the British colonies. It was one of William Pitt's main intentions in the Seven Years' War that Canada should be conquered. He therefore planned a three-pronged attack on French Canada from Lake Ontario in the west, the River Hudson in the south and from the mouth of the River St Lawrence in the east. It was the storming of Quebec by the army of Major-General James Wolfe in 1759 after a difficult landing from the River St Lawrence that was mainly responsible for the successful conquest of French Canada.

The release of the American colonists from the French menace led to criticism of the continued existence of British troops in America and of the taxation that was needed to support them. In the American War of Independence (1776–83), the British redcoats found themselves trying to force the Americans to remain in allegiance to George III and the British Parliament. The Americans had to depend on their own militia, called minutemen because they had to be ready at a minute's notice. Although they were lacking in discipline, they were excellent marksmen. They usually possessed rifles, that is fire-arms with grooved barrels, which were far more accurate than the British service flint-lock. Under the leadership of George Washington and with the help of the French after 1778, the American irregulars won the war. The British army found the co-ordination of a campaign at that distance from Great Britain virtually impossible and two major defeats involved the surrender of British armies at Saratoga Springs (1777) and Yorktown (1781).

The war in India was fought by the East India Company rather than by the British government. The cause of the war was commercial and it was fought between armies that always had a preponderance of Indian native soldiers called sepoys. Conquest of territory was never the object of the warfare, but it became the only way that some Indian princes could be forced to give up the French alliance. There were never more than 5,000 French troops in India, yet French agents had much success in persuading Indian princes to act on their behalf right up to the Napoleonic Wars. As a result of its efforts to expel French influence and maintain order, the Company found itself in possession of most of India.

There were two crucial phases in the Company's expansion. The first was from 1750 to 1760, when there was a determined attempt by the French governor general Dupleix to control the Indian continent. These plans were foiled by the defeat of the French puppet ruler of the Carnatic at Arcot in 1751 and of Bengal at Plassey in 1757. The victory in both cases was gained by a Company clerk turned soldier called Robert Clive. The steadiness and discipline of the Company army was the deciding factor even when the native ruler had a numerical advantage of ten to one as Suraj-ud-Dowlah did at Plassey. The second phase was during the governor-generalship of Lord Wellesley (1797–1805). Not only did he force the remaining pro-French princes to dismiss their French soldiers and to make alliances with Britain, but he also began the disciplining

20 Arthur Wellesley, Duke of Wellington (1769–1852): He developed his military skills in India during the war against Tipu Sultan of Mysore (1798–99) and against the Mahrattas (1803–1805). He was placed in command of a small British expedition which landed in Portugal in 1808. After an initial set-back, he began to use his small army so intelligently that even large French armies could not destroy him. In 1812 he was able to take the offensive and played an important part in Napoleon's defeat. His great victory over Napoleon at Waterloo in 1815 crowned his military career with glory.

of the unruly Maratha rulers who terrorised the Deccan plateau. It was during the Maratha wars that Lord Wellesley's younger brother, Arthur Wellesley, developed his military leadership and showed great aptitude in the art of supply.

Wellington

Arthur Wellesley, later to be made the Duke of Wellington, had already taken part in the war against Revolutionary France on the continent as a lieutenant-colonel. A British army mainly composed of German mercenaries had been sent under the command of the Duke of York, the second son of George III, to help in the defence of the Austrian Netherlands soon after war was declared in 1793. At times, the army fought with spirit and success, but in general the leadership and system of supply was poor. During the bitter winter of 1794–5, the French drove the Duke of York's army across the frozen rivers of Holland until it was evacuated from the continent altogether. Wellington experienced all this before he embarked upon his military career in India.

The French army was very different from the British mainly due to the Revolution. Commanders like the Duke of York and Wellington acquired their rapid promotion by their seniority in the royal family and by purchase, whereas the new French officers gained their positions by merit. In France also there was a system of universal conscription which by 1798 made all single men between the ages of twenty and twenty-five liable to military service. This meant that the French army was a national army while the British army was still a small standing

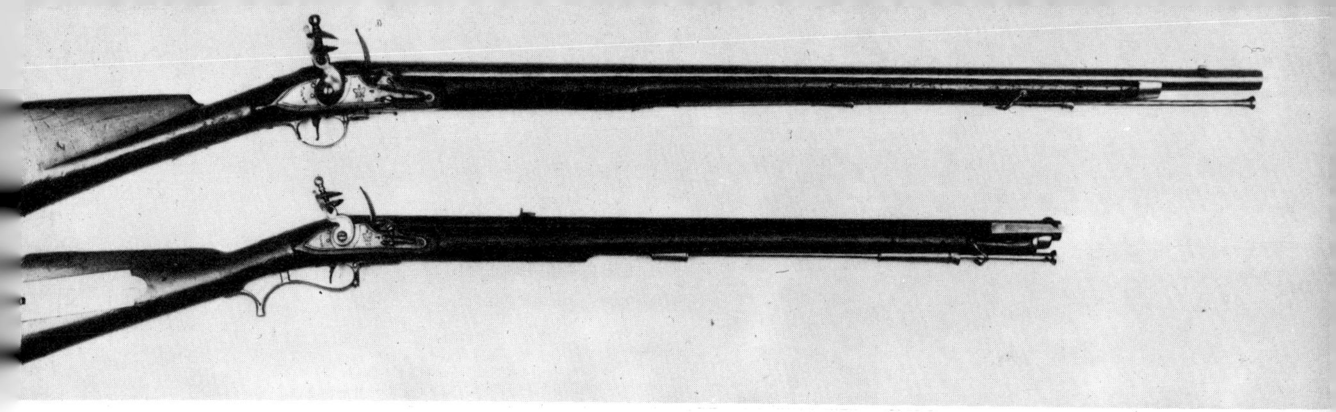

21 A Baker rifle (top) and a Tower Musket. The Baker rifle was the first rifle issued to the British army. It was invented by Ezekiel Baker and was first issued to the British army in 1800. It was with this rifle that Sir John Moore taught his troops to fire accurately. Both weapons have a flint lock mechanism. The flint was held by the beak on the pivot.

army of the old type. The British militia only existed for the defence of the homeland, not for overseas service. At first also the French army was a revolutionary army offering to help neighbouring people to throw off the tyranny of kings and nobles. It was only with the rise of Napoleon and the invasion of Egypt in 1798 that the French army became a blatant army of conquest.

Despite the conservatism of the British military system, change was achieved by the commander-in-chief, the Duke of York, who regularised the system of officer promotion, established the Corps of Waggoners to improve supply and improved the medical service and by Sir John Moore, who developed a brigade of light infantry armed with the rifle at Shorncliffe in 1803 that became the

22 Wellington at Waterloo encouraging his infantry squares which had just resisted the attack of the French cavalry. Kneeling soldiers with bayonets fixed provided a spiny defensive wall for the musketeers standing behind. On the left artillerymen are holding various pieces of equipment needed to effect a shot.

model for all infantry battalions in the army. His troops were trained to have confidence in their musketry and in their captain, so that they could operate efficiently in much smaller units than was usual at that time.

In 1808 a British army landed in Portugal and in 1809 it was placed under the command of Arthur Wellesley, who became Viscount Wellington in that year. Wellington's army never exceeded 80,000, while the French rarely had less than 250,000 in the Peninsula. He therefore had to be careful. During 1810, he built a triple line of fortifications across the peninsula on which Lisbon stood, called the lines of Torres Vedras. The country in front of the lines was cleared so that attackers could neither find cover nor support themselves off the land. At the end of the campaigning season in 1810, Wellington intentionally encouraged Masséna to follow him towards Lisbon, confident that he would be impregnable behind his defences, while Masséna's army starved in their efforts to pierce the defences during the winter.

Wellington was also able to defeat the French army in the field by encouraging it to attack him in favourable defensive positions. In these encounters the French column, which usually won battles by the weight of its attack, recoiled before the steady firing of the British infantry drawn up in long lines, two deep. By 1812, Wellington was able to take the offensive and in 1813 he ejected the French from the Peninsula. A large section of the French army had been tied down in Spain since 1808, partly to deal with Wellington in Portugal and partly to cope with Spanish guerrilla resistance. Napoleon recognised its significance in his defeat, when he called it 'the Spanish ulcer'.

The battle of Waterloo in 1815, which was fought to quell Napoleon's resurgence after his imprisonment on Elba, was typical of British and French tactics. Napoleon attacked Wellington's chosen position on slightly sloping ground in columns after an opening artillery bombardment. The attack was met by a volley and an infantry charge. Before the decisive arrival of the Prussians in the evening, Napoleon used his cavalry in an attempt to defeat Wellington's right wing, but was answered by infantry squares bristling with bayonets on the phalanx principle and grape shot from the British artillery. The small British army therefore redeemed itself before the war ended and played an important part in Napoleon's defeat.

FURTHER READING

C. T. Atkinson, *Marlborough and the Rise of the British Army* (Putnam).
C. Hibbert, *Waterloo: Napoleon's Last Campaign* (New English Library).
P. Young and J. P. Lawford (eds.), *History of the British Army* (Arthur Barker).
P. F. Speed, *Wellington's Army* (Then and There Series, Longmans).

4 Naval Warfare

Trade wars

The battle with the Spanish Armada in 1588 was the first great naval battle between fleets of sailing ships, but it does not mark a turning point in British naval strategy. The fleet of galleons that defeated the Spanish carracks had been steadily improvised from existing ships by John Hawkins as treasurer to the navy for the purpose of cutting the ocean link between Spain and her colonies in America. The galleons were fast-sailing, manoeuvrable fighting ships armed with effective guns that proved superior to the obsolescent Spanish carracks, but there was not enough of them to effect a permanent naval domination of the Atlantic of the kind that was achieved briefly in the seventeenth century by Blake, on a number of occasions in the eighteenth century in the wars against France, and permanently in the nineteenth century. The Elizabethan strategy was to make war on Spanish trade at first unofficially through freebooters and privateers like Sir Francis Drake and later officially as part of Hawkins's campaign to cut Spain's links with her colonies. There were great attractions in this kind of war. It was an outlet for adventurous spirits, it could be justified as part of the

23 The Spanish Armada 1588. Medina Sidonia, the Spanish commander, sighted the Lizard on 19 July. Lord Howard of Effingham tacked his way out of Plymouth with difficulty and followed the Armada up the Channel. The Spanish formed an inverted arc which was very difficult to attack. The only major losses they sustained before reaching Calais were two flagships. Sir Francis Drake was able to capture the ship commanded by de Valdez.

24 Robert Blake (1599–1657). He commanded Parliament's fleet and was one of the most successful British sea commanders of all time. During the Civil War period he was a soldier and only turned to the sea at the end of his life. His greatest triumph was the destruction of the Spanish fleet in the harbour of Santa Cruz (Canary Islands) in April 1657.

religious war against Catholic Spain and there was always a chance of capturing a Spanish treasure ship. Drake's successful capture of a mule-train loaded with silver on the Isthmus of Panama in 1572 alerted Spain to the dangers, and the silver ships were carefully shepherded across the Atlantic in convoys thereafter. Another expedient in the war against Spain was to destroy the Spanish fleet in its harbours as was achieved by Drake at Cadiz in 1587, singeing the king of Spain's beard.

The popularity of the trade war against Spain continued until the Protectorate of Cromwell, when Blake showed both in 1656 and 1657 that it was still possible to make valuable captures and to destroy the whole Spanish treasure fleet. Yet it was quite clear that such warfare against a country's trade routes could never be decisive as a war weapon at a time when virtually all countries could live on their home-produced goods. Since the seventeenth century it has always been Britain's enemies who have resorted to war on British trade as their main naval strategy. The French resorted to these methods in the late seventeenth and eighteenth centuries and captured a vast number of British merchant ships, but it never proved a decisive factor in any war. In the present century, the Germans have twice waged unrestricted warfare on British trade with a similar lack of ultimate success. Experience seems to show that large permanent battle fleets are needed to secure naval superiority and then invasion armies can be supported to fight a decisive battle on land.

The first large permanent battle fleet was provided by Cromwell's republican government and it was then that Britain's power most impressed the continent. It was very expensive to maintain, but its achievements under the leadership of Robert Blake were considerable. Dutch mercantile supremacy was effectively challenged, the North African pirates were punished, British trade routes were

25 The First Dutch War 1652–1654. This illustrates one of the last encounters of this war. It occurred off the coast of Holland and is called the battle of Scheveningen. It was fought between General Monk, another soldier who transferred to the sea, commander of the British fleet and von Tromp, the great Dutch commander. Von Tromp, whose portrait is inset, was killed by a stray bullet during the battle.

kept open and Spain was firmly blockaded all the year round for the first time over the winter of 1656 and 1657. Blake insisted that all his warships should be purpose-built and this tradition was maintained by Charles II after his restoration in 1660. Charles's acceptance of the necessity of a permanent battle fleet marks the beginning of the continuous development of the present Royal Navy. It was Charles who gave it its name and he also gave it a corporate identity by taking a personal interest in its development, an interest that was shared by his brother James, Duke of York, later James II.

Two more wars for mercantile supremacy were fought with the Dutch in Charles II's reign, but in neither of them was there a decisive naval battle. Britain, however, had the geographical advantage in being able to block the Straits of Dover to Dutch trade and during the wars large numbers of Dutch trading ships were captured. By 1674 both sides were prepared to ignore their differences and join in a common opposition to Louis XIV's ambitions in the

26 The Dutch in the Medway, 11 June 1667. This represents one of the great humiliations of the British navy. The Medway flows into the Thames estuary, where the important port of Chatham lies. This port guarded the entrance to London. For several weeks in 1667 the Dutch fleet, led by de Ruyter, was able to block the Thames to British shipping and captured several important ships including the largest ship in the fleet, the *Royal Charles*.

Netherlands. The alliance was sealed in 1688 when William III became king of England as well as ruler of Holland and the United Provinces. There was never any real danger to British naval supremacy in the war with France, despite a setback off Beachy Head in 1690, and by 1702 the Royal Navy was able to support Marlborough's army in the Netherlands without any difficulty. The maintenance of an army in Spain presented more problems as Britain had no naval base in the area. The Portuguese alliance of 1703 opened Lisbon to Britain's use, but even this was too far from the Mediterranean. The capture of Gibraltar by Admiral Rooke in 1704 provided just the base needed as it controlled the entrance to the Mediterranean itself. Before the Spanish War of Succession ended, Port Mahon on the island of Minorca was also captured and both of these ports were confirmed as British possessions at the Treaty of Utrecht (1713).

Eighteenth-century tactics

Since the reign of Charles II, Fighting Instructions had been issued to officers of the higher command based on those issued by Blake in 1654. Their object was to pass on the main rules of warfare so that less experienced leaders would have some rules to apply in conducting a battle. The main rule was that the enemy should be approached from the windward in line-ahead formation so that the guns on the broadside could be used most effectively. This manoeuvre was to be repeated until the enemy was so disrupted that they could be engaged in a close battle called a mêlée.

In the wars with France in the eighteenth century the French ships were, if anything, somewhat superior in design to the British, but their tactics were very timid. The French were generally outnumbered and their main object was to avoid battle where possible. The aim of their gunners was to destroy the sails and the rigging of their adversaries by firing chains, long bars and scrap-iron rather than to attack their hulls with cannon balls. The rigidity of the British rule book coupled with defensive intentions of the French led to some indecisive battles. In these cases the inability of the naval commander to force a result was attributed by the Admiralty to timidity and cowardice on the part of the British admirals, rather than to ill-trained crews, poor ships or the Fighting Instructions.

In the War of the Austrian Succession, Admiral Mathews engaged a Franco-Spanish fleet of equal size to his own off Toulon in 1744. The enemy fleet was in flight and Mathews's signal to his rear squadron was misunderstood, so he decided to engage the enemy before they escaped even though his line ahead had not been properly formed. He crippled the rear of the enemy fleet, but was subsequently dismissed from the service for disobeying Fighting Instructions and for half-heartedness. An even more extreme punishment was inflicted on Admiral Byng, who, in 1756, was sent to relieve the last British-held strong point at Port Mahon, Minorca, which otherwise had been overrun by the French. He had to engage a French fleet equal in size to his own covering Port Mahon. He attacked them

27 Quiberon Bay 1759. This was one of the great victories during the *annus mirabilis*, 'the wonderful year'. It not only led to the destruction of a French fleet but also made their invasion of England impossible. The British fleet was led by Admiral Hawke and his ships can be seen approaching the French in rough line ahead.

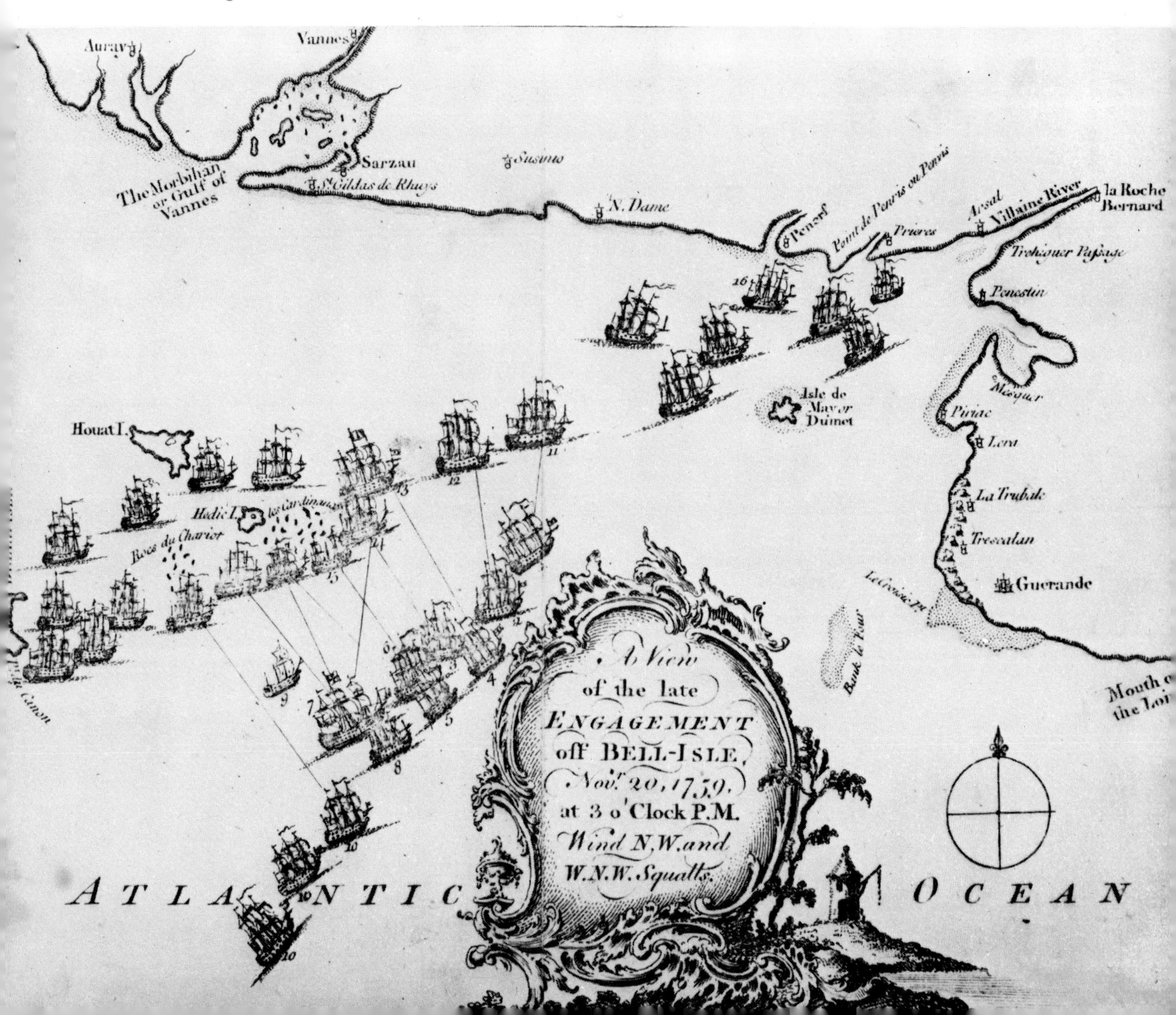

in an impeccable line-ahead, but in the process serious damage was inflicted on his own ships. The French were also badly mauled and withdrew. Byng felt his fleet incapable of either pursuing the enemy or of aiding the British strong point, so he left for Gibraltar to refit. His action was interpreted at his court martial as cowardice, and he was shot on his own quarter-deck.

There was, therefore, a great demand for success in eighteenth-century warfare, and the fate of Byng showed that obedience to Fighting Instructions was not enough. Anson demonstrated how admiration could be won by his fighting circumnavigation of the globe between 1740 and 1744 during the Austrian Succession War when he captured two Spanish ships with treasure worth over £600,000 in the Pacific; he also captured a complete French fleet off Finisterre in 1747. The younger generation of British naval commanders showed similar panache during the Seven Years' War. Two French fleets were preparing for an invasion of England in 1759, one at Toulon in the Mediterranean, the other at Brest on the Atlantic coast. The French navy always had to split its resources in this way to defend all the French coastline and it was essential that the two fleets should combine if the invasion was to succeed. The Toulon fleet was shadowed by Boscawen, the commander of the British Mediterranean fleet, as it passed Gibraltar and was destroyed in Lagos Bay, while the Brest fleet had to escape Hawke's blockade and was chased to Quiberon Bay where it sought haven. Hawke's navigator warned him of the dangerous rocks and shoals guarding the bay. Hawke answered, 'You have done your duty in showing me the danger. Now you will obey my orders and lay me aside the *Soleil Royal*.' In each of these successful battles the tactics employed were a general chase followed by a mêlée in which the initiative was left to individual commanders on the spot. Each proved a major defeat for the French.

Conditions in the navy

In the years of peace which interspersed the periods of war with France between 1763 and 1815, the navy did not maintain its natural superiority either in quality or quantity. In size it needed to be larger than a combination of the next two largest European navies. This proved to be necessary in both the American War of Independence and the Revolutionary War when Britain was at war with France and Spain simultaneously. There was also no attempt to keep together complete crews for the warships in time of peace. Crews were paid off when their ship had completed its tour of commission. Sailors were given a cheque for all the money they had earned during their service and could cash it at the Navy Pay Office in London. Only about 10,000 sailors were kept on naval service in peacetime and this quickly had to be raised to 70,000 or more when war broke out.

The British navy never had complete control of the Atlantic during the American War of Independence (1776–83), when its presence was needed in the Channel, at Gibraltar, in the West Indies and off the coast of North America at the same time. Keppel failed to destroy the French fleet in the Channel in 1778, the French had naval superiority off the North American coast in 1781, and only a victory in the West Indies by Admiral Rodney at the battle of the Saints in 1782 restored any resemblance of British naval superiority.

Matters were little different at the start of the Revolutionary Wars against France (1793–1802), though the dispersion of ships to the colonies was now a matter of choice rather than of necessity. The greatest danger to Britain was presented by the mutinies of the fleets at Spithead near Portsmouth and Nore in the mouth of the Thames in 1797. This was mainly a revolt against the abominable conditions of service by crews that had been forced into service against their will. Pay had not been increased since 1649 when rates were fixed at nineteen shillings (95p) a month for ordinary seamen and twenty-two shillings and sixpence (112½p) for able seamen, despite increases for equivalent shore jobs. The accepted method of recruitment was still the press-gang, whose object was to round up merchant seamen, usually while they were still on board the homebound merchantmen. This was not sufficient to provide a full complement of sailors in wartime and it was then up to the sheriffs in the counties and the mayors in the towns to send recruits, normally from the gaols in their care.

Sailors could therefore have very little pride in the service nor could they derive much pleasure from their work. There was a lack of fresh food in their diet even when they were in port, they were subjected to extremely fierce discipline and there was very little provision for medical care on board ship. In the circumstances the mutinies were conducted in a very orderly way and only at Nore did the demonstration become revolutionary in tone. By May 1797 the sailors had returned to discipline with the promise of improved conditions of service. The enemy gained very little advantage from the disruption as Admiral Jervis defeated the Spanish Navy off Cape St Vincent immediately prior to the mutiny and Admiral Duncan defeated the French-controlled Dutch fleet at Camperdown soon after it finished.

Nelson

Horatio Nelson (1758–1805) made a name for himself at the battle of Cape St Vincent by leaving the line in disobedience of the rules of war, to halt the flight of seven Spanish ships. Though battered in the process, Nelson's initiative enabled Jervis to win a complete victory. Nelson's subsequent naval career involved a series of similar, courageous and decisive actions, which have made him the inspiration of the British naval service ever since.

In 1798, as a rear-admiral in charge of a squadron of thirteen ships, he was sent into the Mediterranean to cover the French Toulon fleet that was preparing for an expedition. It was some time before Nelson discovered its destination after it had slipped out of port during a storm, but he eventually traced it to Egypt. There he discovered it anchored in Aboukir Bay on the Egyptian coast with its flanks safely defended by shoals. Nelson made use of the fact that the

28 Horatio Nelson (1758–1805). Nelson symbolises the dash and courage of British naval officers in the wars against France (1793–1815). He lost an eye while fighting on land in Corsica in 1794 and an arm while fighting on land in the Canary Islands in 1797.

French ships were anchored at one end only, to slip behind the French fleet at dusk and to take or destroy them with little difficulty. The victory gave Britain naval superiority in the Mediterranean and soon after Minorca and Malta were captured as bases for the fleet.

Nelson was second-in-command of the fleet that was sent to Danish waters in 1801 to keep the narrow entrance to the Baltic open to British trade. The timber products from this area were vital in the construction and repair of British warships. In 1800 the Scandinavian countries united in a League of the Armed Neutrality against Britain to stop the British habit of searching neutral ships for contraband. In the Sound it was necessary to destroy the Danish fleet outside Copenhagen as it could effectively block the narrow channels into the Baltic Sea. Hyde Parker thought an attack on the Danish ships too dangerous as they were so close to the shore batteries, but Nelson ignored his signal to return and continued the battle until the Danes surrendered.

In 1805 Napoleon had an army ready to invade England and looked to the

29 Copenhagen 1801. This was the second of Nelson's great victories. He defeated the Danish fleet, guarded by their coastal batteries by bringing his broadside to bear on the enemy in perfect line ahead. The spires and towers of Copenhagen can be seen in the background.

30 Trafalgar 1805. Nelson is seen lying mortally wounded on his own quarter-deck aboard the *Victory*. On 21 October at Trafalgar, he had undertaken to occupy the attention of twenty-two enemy ships with twelve ships of his own, while Admiral Collingwood destroyed the enemy's rear. Nelson took a courageous initiative by leading his ships against Villeneuve's centre. This paralysed Villeneuve's capacity to retaliate but also endangered Nelson's life.

French navy to gain control of the English Channel for long enough to cover his attack. Villeneuve's plan was to draw the British fleet away to the West Indies by pretending that the islands were to be attacked. From Villeneuve's point of view his plan succeeded, but he did not receive support from the French Atlantic fleet which failed to evade the British blockade and Nelson was able to warn the Admiralty of Villeneuve's arrival in the Channel. Villeneuve therefore found his way blocked and found haven in a Spanish port. Napoleon insisted that he should come out and fight and this gave Nelson the chance to defeat the French fleet at Trafalgar. His victory was a triumph for the new tactics which was to break through the centre of the enemy line and then surround the two portions of the opposing fleet. Nelson was almost oblivious to the dangers involved in this close action and was fatally wounded on the deck of the *Victory* while directing the battle. The victory at Trafalgar gave Britain an unassailable naval supremacy which was to be maintained for the whole of the nineteenth century. There were no further major naval battles in which the British navy was involved until the First World War and by that time steam had replaced sail, iron had replaced wood, and rifled guns had replaced cannon. Despite the changes in design and armament, British naval supremacy was greater at the end of the nineteenth century that it had been at the beginning. It was in the early twentieth century that the American, German and Japanese fleets could be considered as potential rivals.

FURTHER READING

G. Callender, *The Naval Side of British History* (Christophers).
D. Divine, *Six Great Sailors* (Hamish Hamilton).
M. Lewis, *The History of the British Navy* (Allen and Unwin).
A. T. Mahan, *Influence of Sea Power upon History* (Sampson Low).
G. Uden, *British Ships and Seamen, Book I, The Ships* (Sources of History, Macmillan).
G. Uden, *British Ships and Seamen, Book II, The Seamen* (Sources of History, Macmillan).
O. Warner, *Great Seamen* (Bell).

5 Nineteenth-century Warfare

The efficient army that Britain had developed during the Napoleonic War was quickly dispersed. It was only felt necessary to retain a regular army of about 100,000 to defend Britain's world-wide interests. Of these, 20,000 were in India as a British force partly financed by the East India Company and partly by the home government, 30,000 manned colonial bases and 50,000 were at home. Although there were 60,000 yeomanry and volunteers and the militia was revived in 1852, they were only for home defence. There were, therefore, no reserves except for a few thousand pensioners and there was no automatic method of relieving overseas garrisons. Some soldiers found themselves exiled abroad on foreign service without hope of relief and as the environment was often very unhealthy, the chance of death from disease was great. Service at home was little more attractive, though the government began to provide barracks. Most of the soldiers' pay was deducted for rations and general maintenance. There was little provision for recreation and wives and children were expected to make a home in the barrack room in an area curtained off from the rest.

There was also little attempt to improve the armament, tactics or administration of the army. The smooth bore flintlock called the Brown Bess was long retained by most regiments, but a new rifle called the Enfield was generally adopted in 1853 in time for the Crimean War. It fired a bullet invented by Captain Minié of the French army in 1850; this incorporated not only a percussion cap in a cartridge which avoided the hazard of damp powder, but also an expansible bullet which enabled the lead shot to fill the rifling and to provide a gas-tight fit. The cartridge continued to be muzzle-loaded. Prestige still lay with the cavalry, though their role in war was now very much as a subsidiary to the infantry. Cavalry officers, who had to be rich to afford the price of their commissions, vied with one another to produce the smartest and best-drilled regiment. The emphasis was on the manoeuvres necessary to make a charge either with a sword or a lance even though this movement was of decreasing effectiveness against accurate rifle or cannon fire. There were also divided administrative responsibilities which had made it difficult to co-ordinate the various services necessary to support an army in war. The Secretary of State for War, the Secretary at War and the Commander-in-Chief were all in charge of different aspects, but no one had complete control of military strategy.

The French impression of Britain's military capacity was summarised by Alexis de Toqueville during the Crimean War in 1855:

> The heroic courage of your soldiers was everywhere and unreservedly praised, but I found also a general belief that the importance of England as a military

31 James Brudenell, Ist Earl of Cardigan (1797–1868). Lord Cardigan was a typical officer of the early nineteenth century, aristocratic, vain and brave. He led his Light Brigade into the Valley during the battle of Balaklava 1854 and reached the Russian guns alive before being taken prisoner.

power had been greatly exaggerated, that she is utterly devoid of military talent, which is shown as much in administration as in fighting, and that even in the most pressing circumstances she cannot raise a large army.

The Crimean War and the Indian Mutiny

These two events revealed the British military situation in all its weakness. France was Britain's ally in the Crimean War, which was fought to contain Russian influence in the Black Sea and Eastern Mediterranean. The main effort was directed against Russian sea power in the Black Sea and the expedition landed just to the north of the Russian city of Sebastopol on the Crimean peninsula in September 1854. War at this distance presented tremendous problems of transport and supply. All the cavalry's horses had to be carried on board ship and it was difficult to foresee all the needs of an army in a colder climate, especially when it was not known how long the campaign would last.

The defences of Sebastopol were very weak and the allies could have captured the city if they had followed up their victory on the River Alma quickly. Delay gave the Russians time to fortify the city, while the Russian field army remained in the open to harry the allied army on the plateau outside Sebastopol. A Russian attack on the British supply port of Balaclava in October 1854 was particularly dangerous. It was the actions in this battle that showed the British Army in all its strength and weakness. The 'thin red line' of Highland infantry stood firm

32 The Charge of the Light Brigade 1854. The valley down which the Light Brigade rode was surrounded by low hills occupied by the Russian artillery. The order which Lord Cardigan acted upon said: 'Lord Raglan wishes the cavalry to advance rapidly to the front, and try to avoid the enemy carrying away the guns . . .' It was not clear what was meant by 'the front' and which were 'theguns'.

33 The Siege of Sebastopol. Sebastopol eventually fell to the allies in 1855. Notice that the mortars and artillery are based on the same principles as their fifteenth century equivalents.

34 The Residency, Lucknow, 1857. During the Indian Mutiny the British community in Lucknow together with 1000 English troops and sepoys were confined to the area round the Residency and were subjected to siege from July until November 1857. The resident, Henry Lawrence, was killed in the first few days, but the remainder held out against 60,000 rebels. This was all that remained after the relief.

in the old tradition, the heavy cavalry brigade drove back the Russian cavalry, but the light brigade, mistaking their orders, charged down a valley into the teeth of the Russian guns and the midst of the Russian army. This was a glorious disaster, revealing all the drilled perfection of the immaculate cavalrymen, but also their stubborn pride.

The winter of that year was a time of great suffering for the allied army which had inadequate warm clothing, insufficient tents and virtually no provision for the sick. For the first time the postal service and the war correspondent of *The Times* made sure that the mistakes and the hardships were widely known. As a result, great efforts were made to improve supply and individuals like Florence Nightingale acted positively to bring comfort to the hospital patients. Sebastopol was captured in September 1855, but the victory was due more to the weakness of the Russian army than to the strength of the allies.

The relative failure of the British army in the Crimea encouraged the Indian sepoys to attempt the destruction of the European armies in India in 1857. There were a number of internal grievances which wrankled, but the greatest temptation to the native soldiers was that they outnumbered the Europeans in the Indian army by five to one. There were 226,000 sepoys in 1757 including 7,000 native gunners and drivers of artillery. In the circumstances it is a wonder that the European troops survived. Luckily the Mutiny was mainly confined to Oudh and Delhi, and the armies in the Punjab and Bengal remained loyal. Another factor was the intense courage of the British troops represented by the long siege endured by the British garrison in the residency at Lucknow under Sir Henry Lawrence and by the storming of Delhi in September 1857 under the leadership of John Nicholson.

One result of the Mutiny was that the government of India was at last assumed by the Crown. From the military point of view, nine white battalions maintained by the East India Company were incorporated into the British army and the number of native infantry battalions was reduced so that the ratio of native troops to whites would never be more than three to one.

Army Reform

A further spur to military reform was the emergence of the Prussian army on the continent as a large and successful new power. By 1870 it had defeated the powerful armies of Austria and France and all European countries studied the basis of Prussian success. Prussia had a system of universal military service under which young men over twenty served for three years with the colours and four with the reserve. By these methods, the Prussians could put a trained army of a million into the field and still leave a militia in reserve for home defence. Another feature was the development of a general staff responsible for planning and administration, which ensured that this huge army could be smoothly and efficiently mobilised and transported by rail to the frontier.

Edward Cardwell, Secretary of State for War in Gladstone's first ministry, 1868–74, had no wish to emulate the Prussian system, but he did seek to remove the anomalies revealed by the Crimean War and to provide the home country with a better organised reserve. He abolished the purchase system by which only moneyed officers could gain promotion and introduced a uniform term of service for twelve years, half with the colours and half with the reserve. The regular army and the existing reserves, both the Militia and the Volunteers, were amalgamated into one united army based on regimental districts. Some existing regiments were linked so they could form themselves into two battalions, one serving at home, the other abroad. They were both based on the same depot which also became the centre for two militia battalions and for volunteer regi-

35 The Maxim machine gun was introduced into the British army in 1891. It was invented by an American residing in England called Hiram Maxim. His guns were manufactured by Vickers and were known by that name as well. Most major powers adopted it as a weapon.

ments as well. In 1881, the local allegiance of the new regiments was emphasised by giving them the territorial titles of counties and other local associations instead of the old numbers. Each regiment had an area for recruitment and a training depot from which the battalions could be constantly replenished. The system was well suited to Britain's needs as the battalion was a useful small unit to dispatch on the multitude of colonial duties that the army had to fulfil and there was always a sizeable trained reserve to meet emergencies nearer home.

There were rapid improvements in small arms at this time. Cardwell gave the army an effective breech-loading rifle, the Martini-Henry, in 1871, and the first magazine rifle, the Lee Metford replaced it in 1888. By the Boer War, the service rifle was the Lee Enfield, which was sighted up to 1,900 yards and with the use of smokeless powder in the cartridges, made accurate marksmanship possible. Ease of loading with these new rifles revolutionised the art of warfare as it was no longer necessary to stand in the open. Infantrymen could now fire and load from behind cover. The Maxim machine-gun introduced into the British army in 1891, began to give the infantry in defence even more of an advantage. The importance of camouflage came to be understood and the Sudan campaign of 1884–5 was the last time that the red coat was worn. It was replaced by khaki on service for both infantry and cavalry. The cavalry managed to keep their lances and their charges until the First World War, but they were shown to be ineffective weapons during the Boer War. The Boer farmers were excellent marksmen with rifles from the saddle and the horse was becoming merely a method of carrying the infantryman into battle.

Colonial expansion

A glance at the roll of honour of a county regiment in a cathedral or church shows clearly the variety of colonial wars in which the linked battalions were required to fight. It also reveals that there was still a greater chance of death from disease than from warfare in the foreign stations. Colonial commitments were nothing new to Britain, but they grew considerably at the end of the nineteenth century when imperial policies were consciously pursued. India had been mainly subdued by the time of the Mutiny, but the conquest of Burma was not completed until 1887, and after that there was still fighting on the North-West frontier of India. The colonisation of Africa involved Britain in a number of new wars against the Ashantis in the Gold Coast and the Mahdists in the Sudan for instance, in addition to the more traditional wars against the Bantu tribes in the south. In almost all cases the British troops were outnumbered, but on most occasions discipline, the Martini-Henry rifle and the old tactics gave them the advantage. There were setbacks such as the defeat of British forces by the Zulus at Isandhlwana in 1879, the massacre of the British forces in Kabul, Afghanistan in the same year (the second Afghan massacre of the century) and the murder of General Gordon at Khartoum in 1885, but in every case the situation was eventually redressed. The rash of wars bred a new type of colonial

36 Canadian troops in action in the Boer War (1899–1902). They are storming a kopje (a small hill). Notice the characteristic sun helmet worn by British troops in South Africa. A bandolier is still worn across the shoulder and a water bottle hangs from the belt.

commander like Sir Garnet Wolseley, Lord Roberts and Lord Kitchener, who were able to adapt themselves to novel military problems with ease.

The most difficult colonial war was the Boer War, 1899–1902. Here the adversary was European in origin, well supplied with arms by European countries and willing to adopt new methods of warfare to defend their independence. The Boers were descended from the Dutch farmers who came resentfully under British rule in 1815. Their descendants had left Cape Province in the Great Trek and found new lands for settlement across the Orange and Vaal Rivers. They had been willing to accept British military aid against the Zulus while they remained mere farmers, but the discovery of gold in the Transvaal had led them to fear British domination of the gold industry round Johannesburg.

The opening of the war showed how ill-prepared the government was for a major colonial war. The towns of Mafeking, Kimberley and Ladysmith were besieged by the Boers and the immediate efforts at relief in December 1899 were so unsuccessful that the second week in the month was called 'the Black Week'. There were under 10,000 British troops in South Africa when the war started and they were surprised by the accuracy of the Boer Mauser rifles and the power of the Boer artillery. In 1900, British fortunes began to improve with the arrival of troop reinforcements and Field Marshal Roberts as commander-in-chief. By the end of 1900, Roberts had driven through Orange Free State into Transvaal along the line of the railway and the Boer State was annexed to the British Empire. President Kruger, the Boer leader, fled to Europe.

The Boer farmers did not, however, give up the struggle. Christian de Wet had not surrendered and he encouraged the Boers to continue their resistance on a part-time basis as saboteurs and guerrilla fighters. Kitchener, who was now

37 Boer commandos in action. Boer means farmer. The Boers were mainly farmers of Dutch descent, who became part-time soldiers. Here they are seen manning the trenches outside Mafeking. Mafeking was defended for 217 days against the Boer siege by Baden-Powell. The relief of Mafeking in 1900 led to extravagant rejoicing in London.

in command, found these tactics very difficult to counter. The number of troops involved was greatly increased and many more of them were mounted to give them the same speed of movement as their enemies. It was found that the only way to overcome enemies that could disguise themselves as peaceful farmers was to destroy the farm houses, place the farming families in concentration camps where they could be closely observed, defend the vulnerable lines of communication with barbed wire and easily constructed block-houses made out of corrugated iron backed with rock, and divide the country into barbed wire enclosures that could be systematically cleared one by one. Although these counter-measures were very unpleasant and unpopular, their successful outcome was a tribute to Kitchener's determination and powers of organisation. The Boers were pleased to make peace in 1902, and they were given a grant to rebuild their farms. In 1910, the old Boer republics were incorporated into the Union of South Africa.

Preparation for War

The Boer War had revealed deficiencies in the ability of Britain to organise a large army efficiently. Cardwell's reforms had produced a military organisation that was very efficient for dealing with small colonial troubles but not with a major war. Another reason for reorganisation was the increasing danger of war on the continent as a result of the aggressive policies of Emperor William II of Germany. The development of a German navy after 1898 was an immediate threat to Britain's invincibility on the sea and a reason for Britain's alignment with France and Russia against Germany. By 1907, Europe was divided into two camps which were arming against each other and Britain had to organise her army with a possible European war in mind.

The reforms of the army are mainly associated with R. B. Haldane, Secretary of War, 1905–12. Before he started his work, a general staff had been formed and the control of the army had been placed in the hands of an Army Council. As a result of the Imperial Conference in 1907, the Dominions formed similar general staffs working in close co-operation with the British so that the armies of the Empire had similar military weapons and outlook. There were also conversations with France from 1906 onwards to discuss possible co-operation in the event of war.

The British army under Haldane's direction was formed into a small highly trained army, capable of moving into France as an expeditionary force at short notice. It was organised into six infantry and one cavalry divisions each with its own staff and supply organisation. The old Militia was transformed into a special reserve to supply replacements for the regular regiments, while the yeomanry and volunteers became a Territorial Army of fourteen divisions and fourteen mounted brigades which was to do some military training each year. Officer Training Corps were also established in universities and schools to provide potential officers with their first taste of military training. These reforms provided at least a framework for the army that fought on the continent in the First World War.

FURTHER READING

B. Bond (ed.), *Victorian Military Campaigns* (Hutchinson).
R. Kruger, *Goodbye Dolly Gray: History of the Boer War* (New English Library).
C. Woodham Smith, *The Reason Why* (Constable).

6 The War to End Wars

A World War was always possible from 1904 onwards. European countries seemed prepared to defend supposed interests in Morocco and more especially the Balkans. Although Britain was in loose agreement with France and Russia, no firm military promises were given or alliances made for fear of provoking retaliation from the Central Powers, Austria-Hungary and Germany. The Germans had a plan in the event of a simultaneous war against France and Russia. This plan had been made by Count von Schlieffen, chief of the German general staff from 1891 to 1906; it involved an immediate attack on France, whom the Germans hoped to knock out in a few weeks before turning to deal with Russia. The actual war broke out in Serbia between Austria-Hungary and Russia in July 1914, but Germany's help to Austria-Hungary took the form of an attack on France. The Schlieffen Plan was to be a scythe-like movement of the German army through Belgium and the Channel ports that would envelop Paris and the French army from the rear. The movement of the main part of the German army into Belgium broke Belgian neutrality, which Britain had guaranteed and the British Cabinet had no choice but to declare war.

The prospect of war was greeted with some enthusiasm in Britain. No one expected it to be a long war and Lord Kitchener, the newly-appointed Secretary of State for War, had no difficulty in attracting volunteers. It was some time before these new recruits were trained and for the first twelve months, the main burden of the war in France was carried by the British Expeditionary Force, which was sent over immediately while the Territorial Force was kept in England for home defence. Military service did not become compulsory for all males between the ages of eighteen and forty-one until May 1916 and the men conscripted in this way were not fully trained for overseas service until the war was virtually over. The war developed into a long bitter struggle and the early enthusiasm was soon replaced by resigned despair. Both the BEF and Kitchener's army were virtually eliminated in the war of attrition that developed in the trenches of the Western Front.

The Western Front

The initial German advance was neither fast enough nor overpowering enough to win the war. The British regular troops surprised the Germans at Mons by the accuracy and intensity of their musketry and the French and British armies were able to defend Paris along the line of the River Marne. As a result of the battle of the Marne in September 1914, the Germans were forced to pull back to a more easily defended line and this line, apart from a controlled German movement back to the even better defended Hindenburg line in 1917, proved

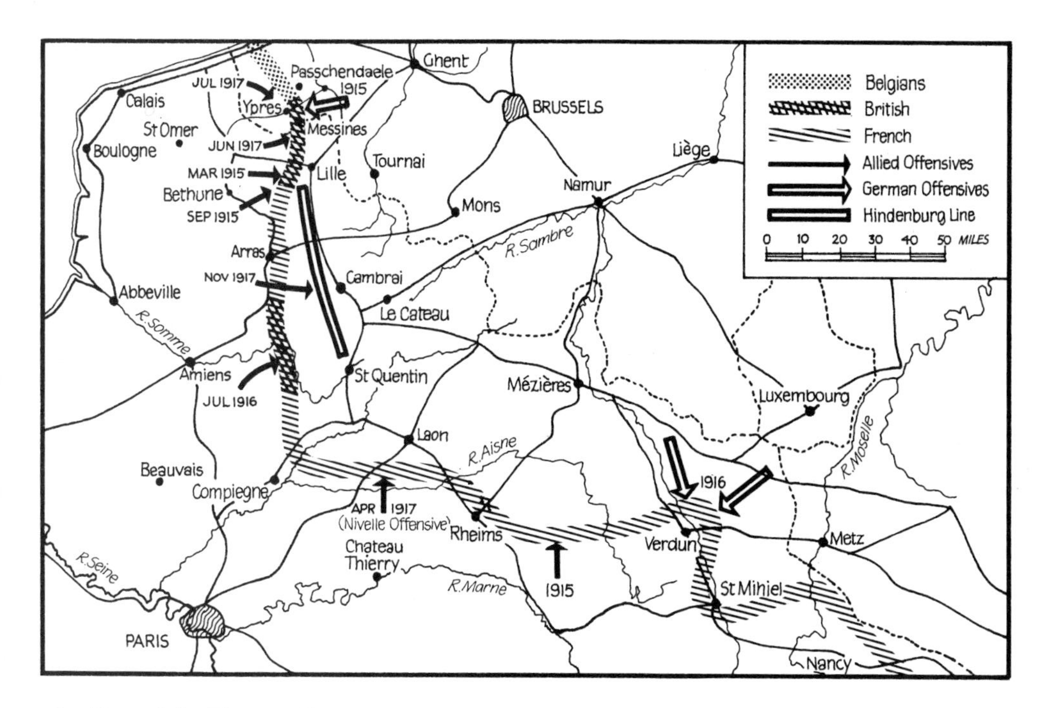

38 Map of the Western Front.

to be the battleground in France for the rest of the war. Trenches were dug in irregular parallel lines, which gave the defences great depth. All kinds of connecting trenches and dug-outs were constructed so that men could survive constant sniping and spasmodic artillery barrages.

In trench warfare all the advantages lay with the defence. There was hope for a time that a constant artillery barrage lasting several days could flatten every trench, cut every piece of barbed wire and pierce every dug-out. This was the basis of General Haig's tactics in the battle of the Somme in autumn 1916, but it proved to be too optimistic. The enemy merely waited until the barrage lifted and watched through periscopes for the attackers to leave their own trenches and then in no time they had manned the craters and mounted the machine guns. Troops advancing in the open were an easy target not only for machine gunners, but also for the enemy artillery. The French army that held the whole of the line except for the British sector from the River Somme to the sea north of Ypres had even more bitter experience of the futility of attack in the defence of Verdun in 1916 and in the Nivelle offensive in 1917. So great were their losses that their army was in a state of mutiny in the summer of 1917.

Life in the trenches was one of extreme futility and discomfort for the soldier. He had to keep continual watch for snipers and enemy patrols, yet could not get comfortable rest when his watch was finished. He had to obey orders that in many cases seemed suicidal and found his enjoyment in the occasional night

39 British and French troops in the front line trenches 1916. The soldier on the left is French. The Tommies (Tommy is a word for a private in the British army) have gas-mask bags round their necks and puttees round their calves, long strips of cloth wound spirally round the leg from ankle to knee for protection and support. Notice the brushwood revetment.

40 Ypres 1918. The Germans remained outside Ypres during the whole of the 1914–18 War and gradually battered it to destruction. This is the ruins of the great mediaeval Cloth Hall. The last Post is still sounded every night at the Menin Gate in Ypres in memory of those who died in the battles near the city in the First World War.

41 The Somme 1916: war in all its horror. Dead Germans are seen lying among debris in Lonage Wood.

patrols into no man's land. The noise from artillery assaulted his ears, noxious smells offended his nose and the sight of death and suffering deadened his other senses. It was no wonder that the soldier's main desire was to escape from it all.

I want to go home
I want to go home
The coal-box and shrapnel they whistle and roar,
I don't want to see the trenches no more,
I want to go over the sea
Where the Kaiser can't shoot bombs at me.
Oh I
Don't want to die,
I want to go home.

When his turn came to leave the trenches for a rest centre in the rear, the soldier didn't have enough energy left to feel happy. In a famous poem called *Dulce et Decorum est*, Wilfred Owen described his unit moving back.

Bent double, like old beggars under sacks,
Knock-kneed, coughing like hags, we cursed through sludge,
Till on the haunting flares we turned our backs
And towards our distant rest began to trudge.
Men marched asleep. Many had lost their boots,
But limped on, blood-shod. All went lame, all blind;
Drunk with fatigue: deaf even to the hoots
Of gas shells dropping softly behind.

Only limited successes were possible in this kind of war and then it was only the result of long preparation. The most dramatic achievement was the capture of the Messines ridge to the south of Ypres by General Plumer in June 1917. Miners drove tunnels under the enemy lines and placed 600 tons of explosive in them. This charge was detonated just before the advance and enabled the British to gain the initial tactical advantage in the battle for this important hill.

42 Passchendaele 1917. Stretcher bearers carry a wounded man through the mud during the battle. The whole area reverted to marsh.

Another limited victory was gained by massed tanks at the battle of Cambrai in November 1917. Tanks had already been used on the Somme in the previous year, but 400 tanks had never been used on one narrow front before. The tanks had compressed brushwood bundles on their roofs to throw into the trenches which might otherwise have been tank traps and broke the formidable Hindenburg Line. So surprising was their success, that sufficient reserves were not ready to exploit the gap.

The most gruesome phase of static warfare occurred to the north of Ypres in the battle of Passchendaele in autumn 1917. This battle was meant to be the opening phase of a thrust which was to capture the U-boat bases at Ostend and Zeebrugge. In fact the offensive became bogged down on the flat land outside Ypres where the shelling destroyed the draining system and heavy rains turned the terrain into a swamp. Haig was very reluctant to call off the attack once it had started and drove the troops forward through the mud to positions where they were difficult to supply. The village of Passchendaele was captured but not the whole of the strategic ridge on which it stood. The only justification for the continuation of this battle which cost the British nearly 400,000 casualties, was that it gave the French time to recover from their mutiny.

The last chance for a German victory occurred in spring 1918. The Bolshevik revolutionary government in Russia that came to power as a result of the October Revolution in 1917 made peace with the Germans. All German military power could therefore be concentrated in France at the beginning of 1918. The reason that they had to win the war quickly was that the United States of America had declared war on them in 1917 and the American army was congregating in France in 1918; in addition the Germans were beginning to experience shortages of food and raw material due to the British blockade of German ports. Ludendorff's spring offensive made some headway but left the Germans holding a very vulnerable salient which Marshall Foch, now the overall commander of the allied troops, was able to exploit in a summer counter-offensive which kept the Germans retreating until they asked for an armistice which ended the fighting on 11 November, 1918.

Weapons

Machine guns had been used in the wars in South Africa but few observers had understood the difficulties that a bullet swept zone would cause attackers in the future. The Maxim machine gun with slight modifications became the Vickers gun which was used in both world wars. It was relatively light and mobile, water-cooled and capable of firing 650 rounds a minute. When it was used in conjunction with barbed wire to slow down the enemy infantry it proved a decisive weapon.

The Germans introduced a new weapon during the second battle of Ypres in April 1915, and this was poison gas. Its use was specifically condemned by the Hague Convention so that its arrival in the allied trenches was met with surprise and dismay. Luckily the Germans were testing its effect rather than using it as the prelude to a breakthrough as it left the Canadians in the trenches absolutely helpless. Subsequently both sides used gas as a weapon and it proved somewhat more effective when used by the allies because winds blowing from the west were more usual in Flanders than easterly ones. The effects of the gas were asphyxiation and blindness, but these could be avoided by wearing gas-masks, which became standard issue in 1915.

Another weapon that became highly regarded as the war progressed was the aeroplane. The Royal Flying Corps was formed in 1912, but by 1914 it was only capable of supplying forty-eight machines with fifteen in reserve to the BEF in France. Within the next four years the number of planes in action increased dramatically and the functions of the aircraft in war became specialised and valuable. Enemy planes presented a much greater threat to the morale of the men in the trenches than the accuracy of their bomb attacks warranted, but General Trenchard took the menace seriously and adopted an offensive policy to force the German planes to defend their own ground troops. By 1916, planes were operating in formations and showed themselves capable of causing destruction in supply dumps and German towns, but only in emulation of similar German attacks on British towns and installations. One of their most important functions was to help the artillery to pin-point their targets.

The German artillery was superior at first both in quantity and quality,

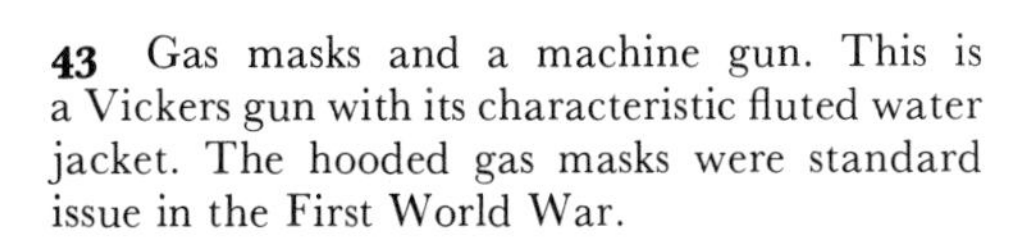

43 Gas masks and a machine gun. This is a Vickers gun with its characteristic fluted water jacket. The hooded gas masks were standard issue in the First World War.

44 British tanks on the Somme. These ponderous machines were too slow and vulnerable to prove a decisive weapon in the First World War. The caterpillar tracks could easily be broken and they become stuck in trenches and craters.

though the French 75 mm gun was reckoned the best of the lighter guns. The importance of medium and heavy guns soon became apparent as a preparation for offensives and Britain soon developed a variety of heavy guns and howitzers. Accuracy and co-ordination became very important as the infantry needed artillery support up to the very last minute before their advance. This was achieved partly by the observation aircraft, partly by wireless and telephone, and partly by the skill of ground observers using sound ranging and flash spotting. Heavy guns were very difficult to move, especially over the ground that they had churned in the bombardment and therefore the infantry could never advance far without losing their gun support. The range of the big guns was around six miles.

The tanks were potentially the best weapon though their slowness made them very vulnerable. Their speed was just over four miles per hour at the end of the war and the heavier version carried two six-pounder guns and four machine guns. The tank was developed in great secrecy and its name derives from the fact that its hull was referred to as a water carrier for Mesopotamia and more briefly as 'a tank'. A medium tank carrying a crew of three instead of the normal eight was also developed and was called 'the whippet'. Both heavy and light tanks were used in the battle of Amiens in August 1918, and their advance was so relentless and successful, that it showed Ludendorff that defeat was inevitable. He described 8 August as 'the black day of the German army in the war'. He went on:

It was the worst experience I had to go through. It marked the decline of our fighting strength and destroyed our hopes of strategic improvement.

The Grand Fleet

The Germans had never expected to outbuild Britain in the naval race that developed in the years before the Great War. They hoped to build a navy of such strength that the greatest sea-power in the world would be so weakened in a naval war with Germany that it would not risk involvement. The Germans certainly achieved this aim by 1914. They had thirteen of the most modern battleships, called dreadnoughts, to Britain's nineteen. Britain had a considerable advantage in medium and light cruisers, but Germany had a corresponding advantage in numbers of destroyers. The balance was too near equality for Admiral Jellicoe ever to want a decisive naval battle. Jellicoe was quite happy to bottle the German fleet within the North Sea. The exit through the Straits of Dover was blocked by the Dover patrol which also shielded the supply route between England and France, while the Grand Fleet was stationed at Scapa Flow, a natural harbour formed by the Orkney Islands. This was a very remote and inhospitable position, but it covered the wide northern passage from the North Sea between Scotland and Norway.

A number of German cruisers were on the open seas when war started and they all caused much anxiety and trouble while they were at large. The *Goeben* and the *Breslau* were in the Mediterranean and made for Constantinople, where their presence persuaded the Turks to join the Central Powers in October 1914. The *Emden* destroyed much allied shipping and port installations in the Indian Ocean until it was destroyed by the Australian cruiser *Sydney*. Von Spee had a squadron in the Pacific which defeated an inferior British force off the South American coast, before it was surprised and outgunned by a hastily gathered superior British fleet off the Falkland Islands in December 1914.

From the beginning of 1915 onwards, major naval action was confined to the North Sea. The Germans had already displayed their freedom within the North Sea by bombarding the ports on the east coast between Great Yarmouth and Newcastle during December 1914, but even these raids proved to have their dangers when Admiral Beatty punished such a raiding party heavily on its return in the battle of the Dogger Bank in January 1915.

The one great confrontation between the two navies was at the battle of Jutland on the last day of May 1916. The new German admiral, Scheer, hoped to tempt the aggressive British Admiral Beatty into chasing a German squadron as he had done at the Dogger Bank and to lure him into the arms of the German High Seas Fleet. Scheer's scheme worked, but when Beatty saw the German Fleet, he turned in supposed flight to draw the German ships away from their base and towards Jellicoe and the British Grand Fleet that had moved towards the Skagerrak. Jellicoe's manoeuvres succeeded to the extent that he placed the British fleet between the German fleet and its base after two short engagements with Scheer's ships. He hoped to be able to block all three possible routes back to German ports after he had lost contact with Scheer during the night, but the German admiral with a little luck, squeezed past the rear of the British line without being noticed. The result of the battle was therefore indecisive. Jellicoe had lost more ships, but his fleet remained intact.

The containment of the German navy within the North Sea proved a serious threat to Germany's capacity to continue the war. Trade with the outside world by sea was very difficult and there was no possibility of overcoming the limitations of German agricultural output by importing food from abroad. The German attempt to win the war in 1917 by unrestricted submarine warfare against British trade was the product of desperation and only served to persuade America to enter the war on the side of the allies. By 1918, the blockade proved the more effective weapon and before the armistice was signed on 11 November 1918, the German navy had mutinied and was in control of the city of Kiel.

World War

The First World War was truly global in its repercussions. The entry of the United States into the war on the side of the allies in 1917 involved a new continent in the war, but already the British Empire and the dominions were willingly fighting for the allies. The German Empire in various parts of the world was unobtrusively conquered by the allies such as Japan. There were also several other fronts in Europe and the Middle East. Some of these were the wars of our allies against the Central Powers such as the Italian front and the Russian front. Others were the concern of Britain and the Empire, who undertook the brunt of the war against the Turkish Empire, which had allied with the Central Powers

45 Map of Gallipoli and the Dardanelles

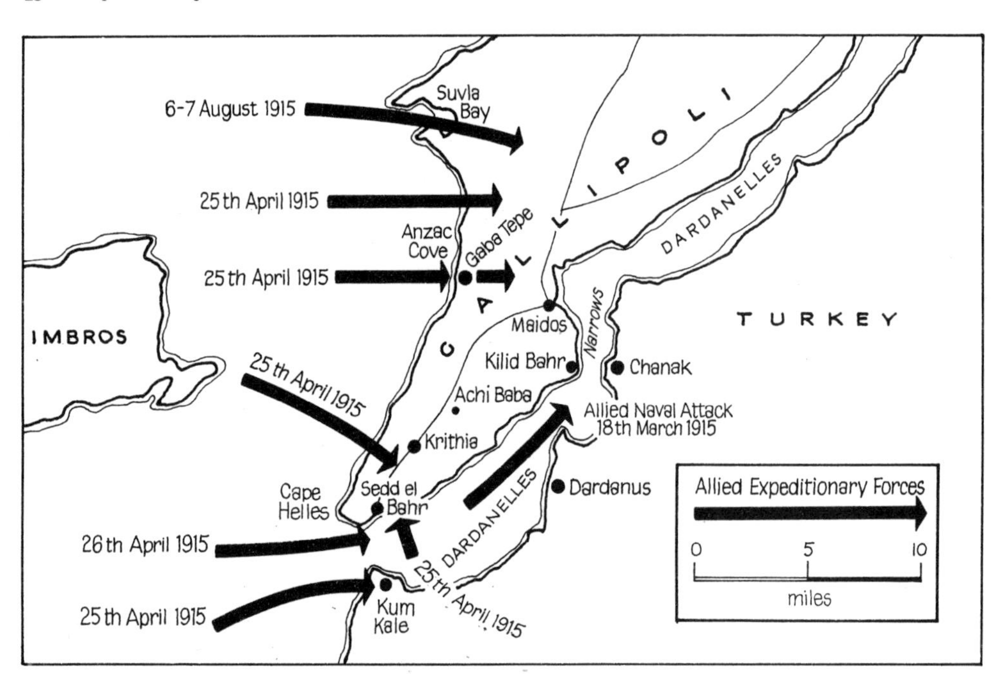

46 Anzac beach in the Gallipoli Campaign 1915. None of the beach-heads on the Gallipoli peninsula stretched much further than the surrounding hills. The beach became congested with stores and the hillsides with shanty dwellings for the troops.

in 1914. Turkey could control major British interests like the Suez Canal and the oil in the Persian gulf, as well as block the southern route to Russia through the Straits to the Black Sea. Britain therefore always took a keen interest in the war against Turkey.

Some felt that Turkey could be eliminated from the war quickly if warships could fight their way through the Dardanelles to the Turkish capital, Constantinople, on the Bosphorus. This was the plan in the Gallipoli campaign of 1915 that began as a naval exploit, but turned into a military expedition when the plan to drive old French and British battleships past the batteries on the banks of the Straits was judged to have failed. Three battleships had been sunk by stray mines in the preliminary entry and though subsequent knowledge reveals that Admiral de Robuck had overcome the major difficulties, he was too appalled by his losses to continue further. In April 1915 landings were made by British, Anzac (Australian and New Zealand) and French forces on the Gallipoli peninsula which, despite subsequent reinforcement, made no progress against skilful Turkish defence. The most successful part of this campaign was the withdrawal of these forces from their impossible positions during the winter with virtually no further loss of men.

The war in the rest of the Turkish Empire was far more mobile than elsewhere. The bad roads and primitive river communications of Mesopotamia created problems of their own. In 1915 General Townshend with an army of British and Indian troops pressed his attack on Baghdad without adequate regard to his supply-route and was forced to seek refuge for his army during the winter in the town of Kut. He was surrounded and when the relief army failed to fight

47 Lord Haig (1861–1928). Douglas Haig commanded the British forces in France from 1915 to 1919. His leadership made a great impression on his generation. When the war finished, he was given £100,000 by Parliament and Bemersyde Mansion by public subscription.

its way through from Basra, he surrendered with his army of 3,000 British troops and 6,000 Indians in April 1916. In Arabia an Arab nationalist rebellion harassed the Hejaz railway from Damascus to Mecca which was the only Turkish link with Arabia. They were helped by a British engineer officer called T. E. Lawrence, better known as Lawrence of Arabia. Eventual success in both Mesopotamia and Palestine came to commanders, who secured their supply routes and bases before moving forward. General Maude captured Baghdad in March 1917, and General Allenby, Jerusalem in December 1917, after they had made this kind of methodical preparation.

Turkey was on the verge of total collapse when the war ended, but like Germany's victory over Russia, Turkey's surrender would have been of little strategic importance. The crucial war was that fought on the Western front. Here the war was one of static endurance with neither side wishing to concede defeat. A clean victory in the field proved impossible: it was just a matter of which side could keep their armies and populations in the war the longest. It was Germany which surrendered first, but British troops had needed a firm reminder of what was at stake in the spring of 1918 during the German offensive. Haig's famous order told them:

> There is no other course open to us but to fight it out. Every position must be held to the last man. There must be no retirement. With our backs to the wall and believing in the justice of our cause, each one of us must fight to the end.

FURTHER READING

C. Barnett, *The Sword-bearers* (Eyre and Spottiswoode).

C. R. M. F. Crutwell, *History of the Great War* (Oxford).

C. Falls, *The First World War* (Longmans).

G. L. Field, *The First World War* (Wheaton).

R. Graves, *Goodbye to all that* (Penguin).

A. Moorehead, *Gallipoli* (Hamish Hamilton).

J. Terraine, *The Western Front* (Hutchinson).

7 The Second World War

The terms imposed by the allies on Germany by the Treaty of Versailles in 1918 were too harsh, humiliating and long-lasting to be tolerated by a great power once it had recovered. While times were normal, world trade healthy and the liberal governments taking root in the various countries of Western Europe, there was a chance that Germany's punishment would be relaxed by general consent. This seemed to be the case when the Rhineland was evacuated by the allied armies in 1930. Matters changed after 1930 when the World Economic Crisis deepened, putting many millions of people out of work especially in Germany and inculcating a mood of bitterness and competitiveness among Germans against the whole non-German world. Hitler's Nazi party became the majority party in Germany and in 1933 Hitler was made chancellor. Once in a position of power, he quickly placed the country under a party dictatorship. Hitler had always claimed that the Versailles settlement was unfair to Germany and he intended to change it. He renounced the disarmament terms in 1933, introduced conscription in 1935, and remilitarised the Rhineland in 1936 without any active objection from the rest of the world. Great Britain had based her foreign policy so much on the collective security provided by the League of Nations, that she was unwilling to act except in conjunction with other League members. In fact, there was a good deal of sympathy in England for Hitler's initial repudiation of the Treaty of Versailles, which many thought was justified. When rearmament was begun in England in 1936, the main emphasis was on aircraft production, but until 1938 the principal effort went into the production of bombers. It was believed that any war that occurred would be in France, that the bombers would always get through in the absence of any effective defensive systems and the best weapon was a retaliatory bomber force. Already in 1936, Air Marshal Sir Hugh Dowding had taken command of a new air defence organisation later to become Fighter Command. A series of Radio Direction-Finding Stations (later known as radar stations), were built round the coast, which provided an early warning system of an enemy attack. All information was sent by telephone to Bentley Priory, the Command Headquarters, and from there orders could be sent to Fighter Sector Stations for action. However, it was not until March 1939, when Hitler threatened an aerial bombardment of Prague, that the priority in rearmament was put on fighter defence. On the military side, conscription was not introduced in Great Britain until May 1939, and then it only applied to young men of twenty and twenty-one who were asked to serve for six months. It was on the day of the outbreak of war that all men between eighteen and forty-one were made liable to call-up.

48 Two generations of fighters. At the bottom is a Spitfire and the next up is a Hurricane. These were the fighters which fought in the Battle of Britain. At the top is a Javelin and below it is a Hunter, both jet planes of the post-war period.

Hitler's annexation of Austria in March 1938 and the Sudetenland in September 1938 had been allowed to pass without retaliation, because he was adding areas of mainly German population; the annexation of Bohemia in March 1939, however, involved Czechs who had no racial affinity to Germans and it was then that the British government began to guarantee a number of Balkan and East European States against further attack. One of these states was Poland, and it was Hitler's invasion of this country on 1 September 1939 that caused Great Britain and France to declare war on Germany two days later.

Dunkirk

Germany had used the years of preparation much better than either France or Great Britain, yet the German army was by no means ready for large-scale war in 1939. The German marshals asked Hitler for more time to build up their armies after the conquest of Poland was completed, while the British expeditionary force of four divisions and the French army formed up defensively along the Belgium frontier, as an extension of the formidable Maginot Line, which already formed an impregnable wall of concrete emplacements along the French frontier with Germany. So little action took place between October 1939 and April 1940 that the period was known as the 'phoney war'.

When the German army did move against Denmark and Norway in April, and against France in May 1940, it was with such speed and precision that the opposing defences were overrun before any retaliation was possible. The Germans had realised that the new weapons, the tank and the aeroplane, made it possible to break through the enemies' defence with the tank and disorganise the rear

49 Dunkirk 1940. Troops are seen awaiting rescue. 338,000 soldiers were taken off the beach in eleven days.

by aerial attacks. The army could then advance by the torrent method with such speed, that the enemy's capacity for resistance could be quickly ended. It was an Englishman, Captain B. H. Liddell Hart, who had preached these tactics in the 1920s, but it was only in Germany that they were studied with good effect. Britain rejected these ideas in favour of the older use of the tank as a general support for the infantry and the British tanks were therefore dispersed along the front. In France, General von Runstedt's army with its armour, broke through the allied line at Sedan, where it was least expected due to the mountainous and forested nature of the terrain in the area of the Ardennes Forest, and reached the sea at Abbeville within ten days. The effect of this brilliant attack was to cut off the defending armies of France and Britain, which had advanced into Belgium to meet the expected thrust from that direction, from the rest of France. When Belgium surrendered, there was no choice for the defenders but to withdraw to the coast, where they were quickly beleaguered by the enclosing Panzer divisions. The defeat of the allied armies on the continent would have been complete had the German attack maintained its momentum after the fourteenth day of invasion. Hitler and von Runstedt halted the Panzer advance at Calais partly through uncertainty in their own total success and partly to allow Goering's Luftwaffe, the German airforce, to have the privilege of delivering the final blow. The eleven days' respite until 4 June gave a scratch assortment of over 800 ships time to carry off the main part of the besieged army from the beaches of Dunkirk. About 338,000 British and French troops were saved in this way. Though they had to leave their heavy equipment behind, the British soldiers represented the cream of the British regular army, whose experience was vital in the training of conscript armies for future battles.

50 Pilots racing to their planes during the Battle of Britain. Churchill said of these pilots: 'Never in the field of human conflict was so much owed by so many to so few.'

The Battle of Britain

Hitler had no prepared plans for the invasion of England in June 1940. The view of Grand-Admiral Raedar, Commander-in-Chief of the German Navy, was that the best proposition was the 'starvation of the British Island empire' by naval and air blockade, seeing that the naval supremacy of the Royal Navy was virtually unassailable. The trouble with this method of siege was that it would take a long time and Hitler was particularly anxious to start his ideological war against Russia and his projected colonisation of the Ukraine, which had been the crusade outlined for the German race in *Mein Kampf*, a book written by Hitler in 1924. He thought that there was a distinct chance that Britain might surrender and that this might be hastened if she was subjected to intensive naval and air attacks and even military invasion. Invasion would only be possible if the German Luftwaffe could achieve air superiority over the English Channel, but if that was achieved, most German military commanders thought that invasion was a practicable proposition. During July 1940 thirteen picked divisions were drawn up on the Channel coast and landing craft and barges began to move towards the Channel ports and Goering, who doubled the roles of political head of the German Air Ministry and nominal Commander-in-Chief of the Luftwaffe, prepared an air offensive.

During July, Goering directed his attacks against the shipping in the North Sea and the Channel, in the hope of luring the British fighters into the effective range of his own Messerschmitt 109s, which were short-range fighters capable of outpacing the British Spitfires. Air Marshal Dowding had no intention of taking part in fighter battles. It was British Fighter Command's intention to husband their resources, to concentrate on attacking bombers and thus force the Germans to use their fighters in an escort role, for which they were not highly suitable due to their limited range. This policy was followed throughout the Battle of Britain and was unpopular with some more rumbustious fighter pilots like Squadron Leader Bader, who wanted a far more aggressive counter-attack. The criticism came mainly from the No 12 Group defending East Anglia and the Midlands, who also felt left out of the main battle, which was borne by No 11 Group under Air Vice Marshal Park. It was No 12 Group who favoured the use of wings of fighters of up to five squadrons to break up the enemy attacks. Yet experience seemed to show that such large wings took too long to form up.

It was on 2 August that Goering ordered the Luftwaffe to destroy the RAF. His intentions were never clear enough in his own mind for him to be able to give his airmen a specific objective for the two-week period that he expected it to take for him to gain air superiority. He did not distinguish between the various branches of the RAF, Fighter Command, Coastal Command and Bomber Command and he also included in his targets the air armaments industry, although it would be a long time before successful bombing here would affect the fighting abilities of the planes in service. The day which began the fortnight of destruction, 13 August, was called *Adlertag* or Eagle Day, and proved too cloudy for successful air operations. At this point Goering had 2,263 planes in service including 702 single-seater fighters, 1,000 long-range bombers, 261 heavy bombers, and 300 dive bombers. Fighter Command had a tactical strength of 666 fighters, but there were nearly 750 planes in reserve. It was not until 19 August that Goering decided to concentrate his whole attention on Fighter Command and it was only on the 24 August that the weather proved suitable for attack on aerodromes. For the next two weeks the Luftwaffe for the first time made progress. They were inflicting about the same losses as they were suffering themselves and in addition, they had done great damage to a number of sector aerodromes in No 11 Group Area. There was a distinct chance that they might knock out all the stations south of London and they were also inflicting unsupportable casualties among the trained pilots, who were Britain's scarcest resource.

The period of severest pressure on Fighter Command's bases came to an end on 7 September, when the Germans transferred their main effort from the airfields to London itself. It was a last desperate attempt by Hitler to threaten Britain with 'the extermination of their cities' in the hope of a surrender. The raid on that day was particularly successful in bombing the dockland and starting numerous fires, but the spectacle still caused Air Vice Marshal Park to confess, 'I said "Thank God", because I realised that the methodical Germans had at last switched their attacks from my vital aerodromes on to cities.' The climax of the battle came on 15 September, when the Germans attacked London twice in one day, but with very heavy losses. This persuaded the Germans that British air power was strengthening rather than weakening and on 17 September Hitler postponed his invasion plan called 'Sealion' indefinitely. In this way he had conceded superiority to Britain's one thousand or so fighter pilots.

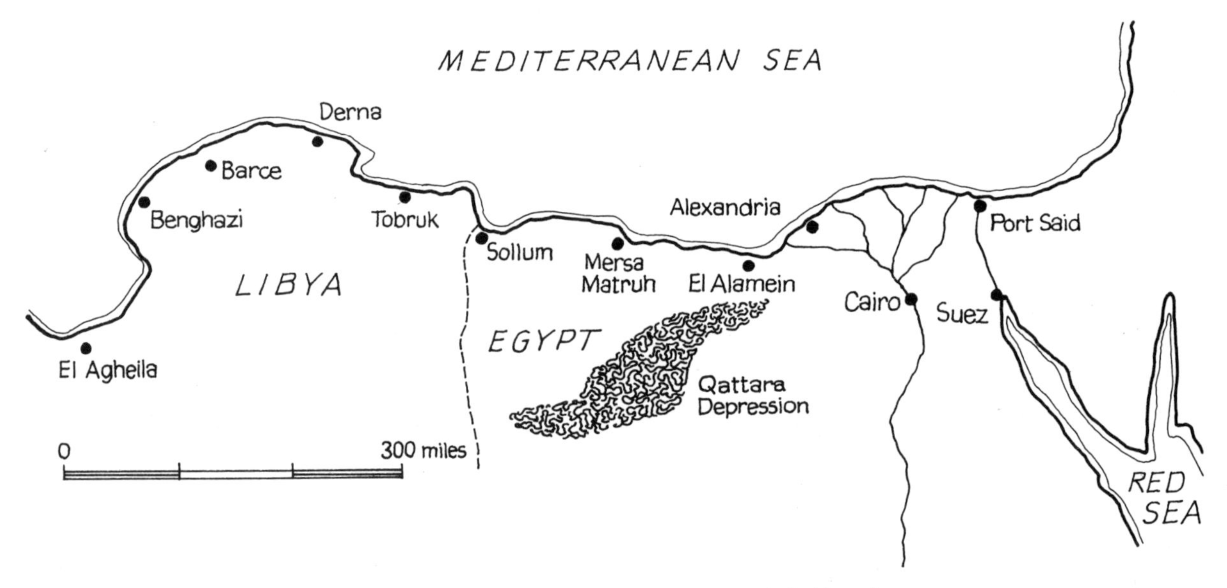

51 Map of North Africa showing the importance of El Alamein.

Mediterranean

During 1940 and 1941, Hitler continued his efforts to force Great Britain to surrender by means of his Blitz on towns and by attacking British shipping in the Atlantic. Meanwhile the British command of the Mediterranean and the Red Sea was threatened by the entry of Italy into the war on the side of Germany in June 1940. By October 1940, British Somaliland had been occupied from Abyssinia, Egypt was attacked from Libya and Greece was attacked from Albania. None of these attacks was sustained and before the end of 1940, a British counter-attack by Lord Wavell in North Africa was so successful that the Italians were driven back to Benghazi. The Italians were also thrown back by the Greeks so it became necessary for Hitler to come to his ally's aid. At the beginning of 1941, Hitler sent a corps of German soldiers under Rommel to stiffen the Italian army in North Africa and planned the conquest of the Balkans. Wavell's resources became hopelessly stretched when he was ordered to detach 60,000 of his troops to defend Greece. Not only was the British army forced out of Greece and then Crete, but also Rommel drove Wavell out of Libya, except for the port of Tobruk that held out bravely.

The outlook for Britain seemed very bleak by April 1941, and it was only naval supremacy that appeared to give Britain a chance of survival. Harold Nicolson wrote in his diary, 'I have no doubt that we shall win in the end. But we shall have to learn the new technique, the secret of mobile warfare, and only when we have learnt it (as we shall learn it) will the efficacy of our sea power be brought to bear.' Before mobile warfare could be practised, it was necessary to supply the desert army with tanks and planes to give it superiority. General Auchinleck, who replaced Lord Wavell as commander of the allied forces in

North Africa in the summer of 1941, relieved Tobruk and conquered Cyrenaica when Rommel was starved of supplies at the start of the German Russian campaign, but this proved only a temporary advance. The Germans mounted a huge attack on the British base at Malta and on allied convoys supplying the North African army in the first five months of 1942. During this period, Rommel was more successful than Auchinleck in building up his strength, though both were under some pressure from their governments to seek a decisive victory. Auchinleck did not want to attack until he had a clear advantage and was quite prepared to allow Rommel to advance deep into Egypt, knowing that he had a carefully prepared line of defence at El Alamein between the Qattara depression and the sea, which could not be outflanked by a tank attack. Rommel's offensive quickly took him up to this line in July 1942, but he left himself with a great supply problem. Before the decisive battle took place, General Auchinleck had been replaced by General Alexander, and Lieutenant-General Montgomery was placed in charge of the Eighth Army. By the time that the allied attack began, as darkness fell on 23 October 1942, Montgomery had a decisive advantage in troops, planes and tanks. This was an advantage not only in quantity, but also in quality, for the Americans had sent 300 Sherman tanks and 100 self-propelled guns, which for the first time gave the troops weapons which matched those of the Germans.

The task of breaking the German defensive line was long and arduous due to frantic German counter-attacks, but when a clear breakthrough was achieved a fortnight after the start of the battle, Rommel's retreat became headlong. Landings in Algeria by the Americans in November 1942, threatened the Germans from the opposite direction and the Germans were gradually squeezed into Tunisia by the two advancing armies. Rommel flew back to Germany, but in May 1942 General von Arnim was captured and ordered the remaining 250,000 German troops to lay down their arms. As the German Russian Army had sustained an equally crippling defeat at Stalingrad in November 1942, Hitler was now driven onto the defensive in every theatre of war. Britain had stood alone against Hitler's Germany until June 1941 and was fighting for her

52 El Alamein, 1942. British troops are dug in before the battle. Only shallow trenches were needed in this mobile war. The standard rifle had changed little since the First World War. The machine gun was now a normal platoon weapon in the form of the Bren Gun, with its characteristic curved magazine.

survival. The turning point came when Hitler took on the two great powers in quick succession. First he attacked Russia in June 1941, then he became involved in war with America when his ally Japan attacked the American naval base at Pearl Harbour in December 1941. In the end it was the mobilisation of the industrial resources of these two countries that made Hitler's defeat inevitable.

Burma

Japan had been expanding her Empire at the expense of China throughout the 1930s and in September 1940, use was made of the fall of France to occupy French Indo-China. These advances threatened British, American and Dutch interests in South-East Asia and they reacted by restricting Japanese trade. Talks were still taking place at Washington in December 1941, when the Japanese decided to solve the problems of naval control of the Pacific by destroying the United States' Pacific Fleet in Pearl Harbour. The attack by 350 carrier-borne planes effected complete surprise on Sunday, 7 December 1941, but they only succeeded in crippling the fleet. Half of the ships, including the aircraft carriers, survived unscathed. This was an important factor, for although the Japanese proceeded to carve out an Empire comprising Burma, South East Asia, the East Indies and the West Pacific in the next three months, the subsequent Japanese advance to the Coral Sea and to Midway Island in May and June 1942 was checked in naval battles, where the most important weapon was the carrier-borne plane. At Midway Island, the Japanese lost four aircraft carriers to America's one, and had to give up the idea of further advance in the Pacific.

The collapse of the British Empire in South East Asia and the East Indies was rapid and complete. The ships and troops lacked air cover and had no choice but to withdraw. Two British battleships, the *Prince of Wales* and the *Repulse*, were sunk off the coast of Malaya, and the British army in Malaya, having withdrawn to Singapore, surrendered. Churchill was very shocked by the loss of this great naval base, telling his doctor, 'I cannot get over Singapore.' Yet the fact was that it was only adequately defended against attack from the sea and there was little to stop a Japanese attack from the landward side. The British fleet in the Indian Ocean had to operate from Ceylon and after an attack on it there, its base was moved to Kenya. Meanwhile the British army in Burma was driven northwards and after a 1,000 mile withdrawal, crossed the border into India.

The Japanese had matters their own way until the summer of 1942. By that time they had conquered most of their objectives and tried to establish a permanent Japanese Empire. It was the British and American intention, while concentrating their main attention on Hitler, not to allow the Japanese to settle. Though there was an American carrier-borne raid on Tokyo in April 1942, the first raid from a land-base was from Chengtu in Szechwan province in China in June 1944. This base was supplied across the Himalaya Mountains from Calcutta and was only maintained with the greatest difficulty. The main task

53 Imphal 1944. This battle was fought against the Japanese in the remote mountainous country on the Burma-India frontier. The troops were adequately supported by light tanks and jeeps.

of the allies was to contain further Japanese advance and to turn back the Japanese Empire from the outer extremities. Great Britain was responsible for the war effort against the Japanese in the Indian Ocean to the west of Singapore.

The main war for Britain was in Burma in the thick jungle on the borderland between India and Burma. The British troops needed to learn the art of jungle warfare and to overcome their inferiority complex in the face of Japanese cunning. Brigadier Wingate helped to build up morale by his excursions into enemy-held territory with a guerrilla army of 3,000 men called the 'Chindits'. In early 1943 they cut railways and harassed outposts, proving that the Japanese were not invincible and that it was possible to supply an army operating in the jungle from the air. The decisive battle in Burma occurred in 1944, when the Japanese launched a major offensive against India. General Slim, who commanded the Fourteenth Army, made great use of air supply to hold his forward positions even after they had been bypassed by the enemy. Two important posts held out at Kohima and Imphal and in the battles for these positions the Japanese had 53,500 casualties to the British 16,600. When the rainy season came with a four-day deluge in June, the Japanese withdrew across the River Chindwin and a great victory had been won. The conquest of Burma took a further year of effort, but Slim had the advantage of numbers and of air superiority as he overcame the frantic and suicidal Japanese resistance. In March 1945 he won the important battle for Meiktila which forced the Japanese to surrender Mandalay and in May 1945, Rangoon was recovered.

Burma was only one small theatre of the war against Japan. The brunt of the attack was carried by the Americans, fighting their way from island to island in the Pacific. By the middle of 1944, they had island bases for their planes within range of Japan and it was from the air that the decisive attack was to be made.

Europe

It had been hoped that the 'Torch' landings in Algeria in November 1942 would have ejected the Axis powers from North Africa by the end of the year so

54 D-Day, 6 June 1944. Canadians are seen landing from improvised ships. Their mode of transport gives some idea of the variety of ideas that were used to move rapidly inland.

that landings could be made in Europe in 1943. Stalin was particularly keen that a 'second front' should be opened as soon as possible, but he was disappointed at the Casablanca Conference in January 1943, when the allies announced that a landing on the Atlantic coast of France would not be made until 1944. Their plan for 1943 was an invasion of Sicily and Italy. Despite the capitulation of Italy in September 1943, the Italian campaign was slowed down by well-organised German defence just north of Naples during the winter. Rome was not reached until June 1944, by which time the allied army was landing in Normandy, Churchill, who favoured the Mediterranean fronts, but who would have preferred landings in the Balkans to landings in Italy, had described this area as the 'soft underbelly of the Axis'. The long fight through Italy that continued for the rest of the war proved that it was anything but soft. The mountainous terrain, commanding the roads from north to south, gave the Germans commanding positions across the peninsula.

While the operation for landing an army in Normandy, called Operation 'Overlord', was being prepared, the Germans had to keep a large part of their army to guard the Atlantic coast. In addition, two-thirds of the German air force and almost all her effective naval force were operating in Western Europe, so it is not quite true to say that Stalin was bearing the whole weight of German power until June 1944. The Normandy landing was carefully prepared. Elaborate attempts were made to lead the Germans to expect an attack at Calais; mock landing craft were assembled in ports in that area and the enemy was fed with rumours through secret service channels. An invasion fleet of 7,000 craft had to be assembled to take eight divisions across the considerable stretch of water. Calm seas were vital and General Eisenhower had to wait for gales and storms to subside before ordering D-Day on 6 June. The landings were made by sea and from the air and the German Atlantic wall of defence was breached effectively along a fifty mile front. Within thirty days, one million men and three-quarters of a million tons of supplies were landed in France. A special 'Mulberry' harbour was built by towing concrete caissons across the Channel and sinking them end to end to form piers. A special flexible pipe called Pluto was also laid across the Channel so that oil could be pumped straight across. Hitler was taken by surprise by these landings, but soon brought his armour to bear against the British bridgehead in the vicinity of Caen. The Americans to the west, however, were able to capture the Cotentin Peninsula with its port of Cherbourg and within

55 This is an improved version of the German V1 flying bomb which was captured by the advancing British troops before the Germans had a chance to use it. The V1 or doodlebug was pilotless. This version was to have been piloted as a flying bomb. The pilot would have baled out before impact.

two months they broke through, advancing first south then north to join up with the British. The move threatened to surround a considerable German army, but most of the Germans managed to avoid the trap. Montgomery's army now swept north to capture the Channel ports, while General Patton freed Paris and moved on towards Germany. Montgomery tried to persuade Eisenhower, who was overall commander, that a single thrust into Germany would end the war more quickly, but Eisenhower diplomatically decided that an advance should be made on a broad front. One strong reason for a rapid advance into the Low Countries was the destruction of the flying bomb bases, which were bombarding London. Montgomery's plan in September to leap-frog the Maas and the two branches of the Rhine by dropping paratroopers to seize the bridges went awry at Arnhem in the north. A Panzer Division and Model, the new German commander in the West, were both close at hand and after days of bitter fighting, the surviving British and Polish troops had to escape back to the allied lines, which had safely incorporated the other two bridges. Another setback which delayed the defeat of Germany until 1945 was the desperate counter-attack that von Runstedt made in the Ardennes during the winter. It was a desperate gamble to repeat the original breakthrough that the Germans had achieved in 1940, but this time the thrust was soon contained by Montgomery, who was content to see the Germans wasting their resources in costly attacks.

The crossing of the Rhine was achieved on a broad front in March 1945, and there was then little that the Germans could do to defend their country, as they had to face a similar invasion from the Russians in the East. On 30 April 1945, Hitler committed suicide in Berlin and on 4 May, Admiral Doenitz, the new German leader, surrendered unconditionally at Montgomery's headquarters on Luneburg Heath.

The German brand of mobile warfare, which was closely emulated by the Japanese in 1942, only succeeded when the attack enjoyed superiority in the air and at least equality in armaments. By the end of 1942 the Germans were surrendering control of the air and about the same time, though their munitions production was increasing through the energy of Albert Speer and the relative ineffectiveness of allied bombing, there was no chance of Germany keeping pace with American, Russian and British industrial production combined.

FURTHER READING

F. de Guingand, *Generals at War* (Hodder and Stoughton).
G. Evans, *Slim as a Military Commander* (Batsford).
H. A. Jacobsen and J. Rohwer (eds.), *Decisive Battles of World War II: The German View* (Deutsch).
K. Savage, *The Story of the Second World War* (Oxford).
R. R. Sellman, *The Second World War* (Methuen).
P. Young, *World War 1939–45* (Barker).

8 Total Warfare

Britain is very fortunate that there has never been a successful foreign invasion since the Norman Conquest of 1066. There was the landing of William of Orange in 1688 to claim the throne, but this was in no sense an enemy occupation. During the last 900 years, British civilians have never had to suffer the depradations of marauding foreign soldiers, except for those disturbed by coastal raids. Before the twentieth century, war had affected only a small number of people fighting in the army and the navy. Matters changed in the First World War when virtually the whole population had to mobilise themselves for war. So many men were needed at the battlefront, that women had to take on men's jobs in the factories. Attacks on merchant shipping by U-boats led to shortages of food, and cities experienced their first taste of bombing. This method of warfare, mainly directed against civilians, was pursued even more wholeheartedly by the Germans in the Second World War, when towns were bombed indiscriminately. The British followed similar policies in their blockade of German ports in the two wars and in their inaccurate 'carpet' bombing of German towns. Winston Churchill's summary of the change in warfare was that

> . . . war, which used to be cruel and magnificent, has now become cruel and squalid. . . . Instead of a small number of well-trained professionals championing their country's cause with ancient weapons and a beautiful intricacy of archaic manoeuvre . . . we now have entire populations, including even women and children, pitted against one another in brutish mutual extermination. . . .

Bombing

Bomb attacks on Great Britain began in the First World War in a German effort to demoralise the civilian population. The first raids were by Zeppelins but plane attacks soon followed. London experienced a number of attacks and

56 A Zeppelin. This shows a German Zeppelin about to ascend from her base for a raid on London during the First World War. There were twelve Zeppelin raids on London during the war, apart from aeroplane raids. Zeppelins proved rather vulnerable to air attack and were likely to be shot down in flames.

57 Bomb damage. This photograph was taken on 28 September 1940 in the East End of London at the beginning of the Blitz. A Heavy Rescue group is searching the wreckage for survivors. Members of the ARP stand by giving advice.

during a raid by fourteen twin-engined Gothas in June 1917, 162 people were killed. These raids created great terror, but they were to be but a foretaste of the long bombardment that Britain experienced in the Second World War.

Hitler's air attacks in 1940 began as a strategic exercise against the Royal Air Force, and in September 1940 degenerated into a campaign to undermine civilian morale and to force Britain's surrender. The Blitz on London began with a day and a night raid on Saturday, 7 September, which concentrated on the London Docks and started huge fires. A. P. Herbert, who was a Member of Parliament living on a boat in the Thames described the scene that night. 'We rounded Limehouse Corner and saw an astounding picture. Half a mile of the Surrey Docks . . . was ablaze – warehouses, wharves, piers, dolphins, barges. The wind was westerly, and there was a wall of smoke and sparks across the river. Burning barges were drifting everywhere . . . we put wet towels round our faces and steamed at half-speed into the torrid cloud. Inside the scene was like a lake in Hell.' At this time night fighters had no radar and therefore had little chance of intercepting the enemy. Complaints by civilians that they seemed to have no cover led to the withdrawal of night fighters and their replacement by an anti-aircraft barrage at night. The guns were relatively ineffective and the shrapnel from the bursting shells was dangerous to the people down below, but their presence and noise was reassuring to flagging morale. London was raided for seventy-six consecutive nights except for 2 November and the main burden was carried by the East End near to the docks. Fewer people were killed outright by the raids than had been expected, but the problems of rehousing the homeless was on a scale that had not been foreseen. Unexploded bombs meant that large

58 Bomb damage. The two most devastating raids of the war were those on Dresden 14 February 1945 and Hiroshima 6 August 1945. Both were cases of indiscriminate bombing of civilian targets and each killed about 100,000 people. As can be understood, it is virtually impossible to count dead when faced with this kind of destruction. The picture at the top is of Dresden; the bottom is of Hiroshima.

areas had to be evacuated and all kinds of temporary arrangements had to be made for the suffering people. Rest centres had to be improvised and field kitchens constructed. Voluntary service organisations worked unselfishly throughout the crisis and the government soon saw that house repair would have to be made a high priority.

During October 1940 the weight of the Luftwaffe attacks shifted to the provinces. On 14 November 1940, Coventry suffered an attack which became the model for a number of attacks on provincial centres, which were described as 'coventration'. Coventry was attacked with incendiary bombs followed by high explosive bombs in a ten-hour raid which virtually destroyed the city centre and wrecked a third of the city's houses. The cathedral was burnt to the ground and the whole area, which was a centre of war production, was stunned. In the following months other cities like Bristol, Plymouth, Belfast, and Clydebank in Glasgow, suffered similar devastating attacks. In May 1941 the Luftwaffe also concentrated on the Western ports before directing its attention to Russia. From summer 1941 onwards raids became much more sporadic. Hitler ordered a series of raids on cathedral cities and places of historic interest like Exeter, Bath and York in 1942 in retaliation for raids by Bomber Command on the medieval Baltic ports of Lubeck and Rostock in the spring of that year. There was also a temporary resumption of the air attacks on London in early 1944, which was called 'the Little Blitz'.

In June 1944 the Germans launched a new weapon called the V1, which was a pilotless aircraft full of explosive that became known as 'the flying bomb' or 'the doodlebug'. About 100 of these were launched towards England each day from bases on the continent so that they would plummet to the ground when their fuel ran out. It was soon realised that there was little virtue in shooting down these rather predictable targets overland, so all the anti-aircraft guns were massed on the coast and proceeded to destroy about half of these missiles over the sea. Yet another weapon was introduced in September 1944 in the form of the V2, a rocket which gave no warning of its arrival. It was fortunate that these were used by the Germans late in the war as there was no means of combatting them except to deprive Germany of the territory in Holland from which they could be launched. V1s and V2s killed about 9,000 civilians and certainly disturbed the peace of mind of London's population while they lasted.

The bomber attack on Lubeck in March 1942 inaugurated the second Bomber Command offensive on Germany. This aimed to break the morale of the enemy civil population and in particular industrial workers, even if it only meant destroying their homes. The first offensive against German towns in 1940 and 1941 had been made in night raids without command of the air, without the necessary equipment for precise bombing and at the expense of heavy casualties among the pilots. Nonetheless, there was still great confidence in the ability of Bomber Command to win the war on its own. Raids like the thousand bomber raid on Cologne in May 1942 were expected to be too much for the civilian population to endure, but such forecasts proved wrong. The German government provided adequate shelters in the most vulnerable towns and survival was possible in the face of the most dreadful raids. Accuracy improved in 1943 when an elite pathfinder force was sent ahead of the raid to mark the target with flares, but Air Chief Marshal Harris, head of Bomber Command still expected to win the war by weight. He told Churchill in November 1943, 'We can wreck Berlin from end to end if the USAAF will come in on it. It will cost us 400–500 aircraft. It will cost Germany the war.' In 1944 the bombing effort was increased with the American Army Air Force (USAAF) bombing by day and the RAF by night. Even this offensive had no great success until the introduction of the American 'Mustang' as a long-range fighter capable of dominating the air space over the targets. At the end of the war the bombing attacks were devastating and in the case of the raid on Dresden in February 1945, led to the worst casualties of the war. Dresden was subjected to a firestorm raid in 1945, although it had no previous experience of heavy raids and therefore did not have adequate deep shelters to escape the intense heat. As a result, approaching 150,000 people died during the one raid. Before the end of the war, as great a weight of bombs was being dropped on one German city in one day as had been dropped on London in the whole course of the war. In the circumstances, British suffering from bombing must be judged moderate in comparison with that of the Germans. Bombing by both sides became indiscriminate and in neither case did it undermine the country's willingness and ability to fight.

Blockade

Since the beginning of the nineteenth century it has been tempting for Britain's enemies to seek victory by depriving her of the raw materials for her industry, the outlets for her trade and more recently, the food for her large population, by attacks on her merchant shipping. France attempted to deprive Britain of her markets during the Napoleonic War by closing all the continental ports under French control to British trade, but the effect on British industry was slight. In the First World War, Admiral von Tirpitz directed the German submarines called U-boats against English merchant ships in the Atlantic Ocean as a reprisal against the British blockade of German ports. At first the Germans tried to distinguish between British and neutral ships, but in 1917 they began unrestricted U-boat warfare against all shipping. During the second quarter of 1917 the U-boats presented a very real threat to British trade for allied shipping losses were three times greater in tonnage than ships being built. The adoption of a convoy system for inward ships in May 1917 and for outward ships in August 1917 greatly reduced the number of losses and by 1918 the crisis had passed.

Convoys were organised from the beginning of the Second World War, but it was some time before they gave adequate protection to the slow cumbersome merchant ships. At first, adequate escort ships were not available and the navy

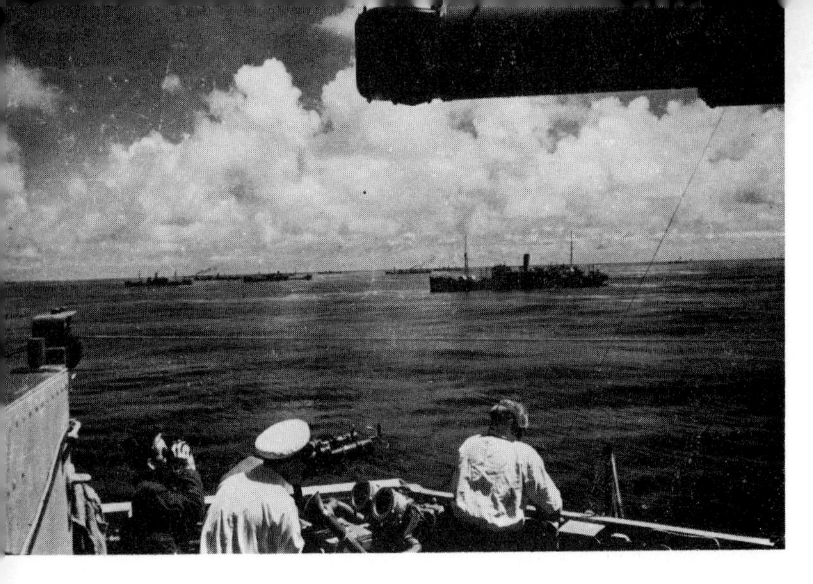

59 A convoy in the Mediterranean 1943. This picture is taken from an escort cruiser on 11 September 1943. The sailors on the bridge scan the sky carefully while the merchant ships continue on their journey.

was very grateful for the loan of fifty old American destroyers in September 1940. It was not until the summer of 1941 that the increasing availability of escort vessels allowed a continuous escort to be given to Atlantic convoys during the whole voyage from America. The importance of air support was also gradually conceded and in April 1941 Coastal Command aircraft were detailed to naval escort duties. Planes operating from Great Britain, Iceland and Newfoundland could cover all but the middle of the Atlantic Ocean. This gap was filled where necessary by fighters catapulted off escort ships and finally by escort aircraft carriers.

The battle of the Atlantic continued for forty-five months until the end of May 1943, when Admiral Doenitz conceded that the convoys were too strongly defended and withdrew his U-boat packs from the North Atlantic area. Up to this point, the U-boats had been destroying allied shipping at a faster rate than it could be replaced, and the German Admiralty had been gradually increasing the number of U-boats on the seas. The Germans began the war with only twenty-two ocean-going submarines ready for service, yet they succeeded in sinking 800,000 tons of shipping in the first nine months. The German 'happy time' was from July 1940 to March 1941. During this period after the fall of France in June 1940, U-boats could operate from French ports and found easy targets near the Irish coast. Thereafter the British convoy system was efficient and the U-boats were not to meet with such easy targets again until the entry of America into the war in December 1941. By the summer of 1942, American trade had been organised into convoys and the Germans had to make a decisive bid to win the battle in the mid-Atlantic where the convoys had least air cover.

U-boats waited on the convoy routes and signalled U-boat Command when a convoy was sighted. A pack of U-boats was then ordered to the area to make a concerted attack. The high frequency transmissions between U-boat and base could be picked up by direction-finders on shore and in 1941 by escort ships as well. The convoys therefore had warning of attack. If planes with radar were in the area, an even more accurate position could be given if the U-boats were surfaced as they often were for recharging their batteries. It was only towards the end of the war that the schnorkel was fitted, allowing U-boats to recharge under water. Underwater detection was possible by means of a sonar device called Asdic, which was fitted to escort ships. Good teamwork and a combination of these detection systems gradually gave the escort an advantage over the U-boats, which were hunted and then sunk with depth charges or by ramming.

German surface ships were also a hazard to merchant shipping from time to time. Battleships and cruisers slipping out into the Atlantic from German ports were particularly troublesome on the Atlantic in 1941. It led to epic engagements like that of the battleship *Bismarck*, which was chased and finally sunk in May 1941. The worst losses on one convoy, however, was on the PQ17 bound for Russia by way of the North Cape, when twenty-three out of thirty-four ships were lost. This convoy, on a very hazardous route, was ordered to scatter because it was feared that the German battleship *Tirpitz* was about to attack. The single ships then became easy targets for U-boats. Merchant seamen were in the very front-line of the war and 33,000 of them lost their lives. The effect of these shipping losses on life in Britain was to create shortages of many products, in particular food.

Civilian participation

In both the First and the Second World Wars the civilian population was called upon to make a full contribution to the war effort and was forced to suffer the hardships caused by enemy raids and food shortages. A typical list of requests appeared on a poster early in the Second World War. People were asked

to eat National Wholemeal Bread
not to waste food
to keep the children in the country
to know where your Rest Centre is
to know how to behave in an air raid shelter
to look out in the blackout
to look for poison gas
to carry your gas masks always
to join the AFS (Auxiliary Fire Service)
to fall in with the fire bomb fighters
to register for Civil Defence duties
to help build a plane
to recruit for the Air Training Corps
to save for Victory

Everyone in the cities would have considered sending their children away to the country as evacuees during the summer of 1939 and about three-and-a-half million children were actually evacuated. These children left their mothers and fathers and went off to the country with their school. Many evacuees drifted back during the 'phoney war' period when the expected raids did not materialise,

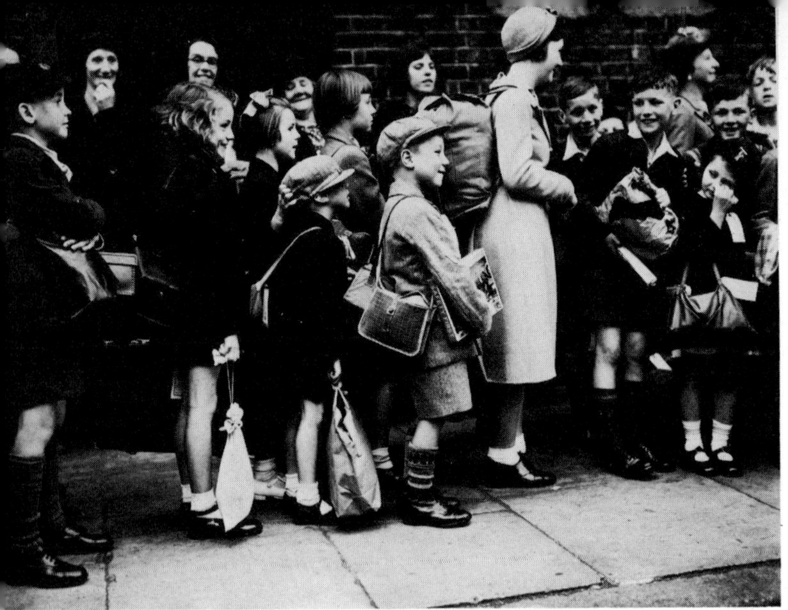

60 Evacuation. This group of children waited to be evacuated from London in June 1940. Many London children benefited enormously from the fresh air and better food of the countryside, but these children seem to be smart, clean and well nourished before they left.

but many stayed away for the duration of the war. Rationing was introduced in 1940, as it had been previously in a rather half-hearted manner in 1918. The Ministry of Food issued ration books and kept a firm control over the importation and distribution of food throughout the war. One of their innovations was the National Loaf, which was grey in colour, but had much better nutritional qualities than the white loaf. Other ways in which the government tried to make sure that the people had a balanced diet was through the non-profit making British Restaurants run by local authorities and by the education of housewives in the provision of a balanced diet in the radio programme 'Kitchen Front'. The government also distributed leaflets to encourage the 'Dig for Victory' campaign so that the men would produce more vegetables in their gardens and allotments. Everyone was continually badgered into saving their money by putting it into National Savings so that it became a national obsession. Weekly savings news was published on the radio and there were frequent special weeks like 'Wings for Victory' or 'Salute the Soldier'. All these efforts were on a far greater scale than in the First World War and illustrate the growing involvement of the average citizen in the war effort.

There were many specific jobs in connection with the war which civilians fulfilled. In the case of men there was no compulsion in the recruitment for quasi-military duties like home defence and air-raid wardens from among those who were not eligible for conscription, and very little direction of labour to vital work. Female labour, however, was required badly to compensate for the great shortage of male labour in the service industries like milk delivery, bus driving and railway work due to the loss of men to the forces and munitions work. Unmarried women between the ages of twenty and thirty were conscripted in December 1941, and by 1943 all unmarried women were termed 'mobile', making them liable to be drafted to any part of the country where their labour was needed. Some of these were sent into the Women's Land Army, whose uniform of green jerseys and brown breeches was a common sight during the war period. The mobilisation of women had occurred on the same scale but

61 The Home Guard. Over one million men had enrolled in the Home Guard by the summer of 1940. This group were members of the LCC Home Guard employed at County Hall, London. They provided guard for the Main Entrance of the building.

in a different way in the First World War and therefore the wars have contributed more than anything else to the full participation of women in the working life of the community.

Those men who were not conscripted into the forces had plenty of opportunity for service at the beginning of the war. The Air Raid Precaution service (ARP) was developed well before the war started in 1937 to be ready for the heavy surprise air raids that were thought possible. The ARP was actually mobilised in September 1938 and at the same time thirty-eight million gas masks were issued as war seemed so imminent. In this way a system of air raid wardens was already in existence when war started. The warden's duty was to lead and advise his neighbours in the event of air raids and call up help from the Civil Defence rescue services or local fire services if need arose. During the period of the Blitz the work of all these volunteers, some full-time, some part-time, was taxing and exciting, but as the raids died down it entailed long periods of monotonous waiting.

Another important service was the Home Guard, which was originally called the Local Defence Volunteers. It was mainly responsible for the hurried preparation of defences in 1940. Anti-glider devices were erected on the fields and anti-tank traps along the sides of the roads. At first, the one-and-a-half million members of the Home Guard were recruited from among the veterans of the First World War, but youngsters began to join, so that by 1943 the average age was below thirty. By that time the danger of invasion had passed, but they were taking over some of the anti-aircraft batteries from the regular soldiers. J. B. Priestley, a popular broadcaster during the war, said of these organisations, 'it has been found necessary to bring into existence a new network of voluntary associations such as the Home Guard, the Observer Corps, all the ARP and fire-fighting services, and the like. . . . They are a new type, what might be called the organised militant citizen.' It was also conceded that the citizens who had contributed so fully to the war, would expect a society which cared for all its members after the war was over.

62 Women war workers. This photograph was taken in 1916 and shows women working in a lens factory.

Social effects

Both wars had permanent social and political results. In the First World War the contribution of women to the war led to the concession of the woman's vote in 1918 and there was an expressed desire to build 'a fit country for heroes to live in' from Lloyd George in the 1918 Election. Little progress was made towards giving the ordinary man a secure job, let alone a pleasant home and a good standard of living. The permanent rate of unemployment in the twenty years between the wars was so high that it was seriously wondered whether the common man had a status in the country that was worth fighting for in the Second World War. Nothing made the more affluent parts of the country more aware of the poverty prevalent in the cities than the evacuees who arrived in their midst in 1939. Not only did the children often have lice and impetigo, but also in some cases they were not in the habit of using toilets. Many were not used to baths and the condition of their clothes and shoes was appalling. In most cases it was the country poor who housed the city children over a long period, but many willing middle-class homes had received children, only to realise that the habits of the city child were not compatible with their way of life.

Another great change caused by the Second World War was to create jobs for every person who was capable of working. A manpower shortage was evident by the middle of 1940, and a Manpower Requirements Committee was established to make sure that at least the essential industries were fully manned. The dignity of earning a week's wage was enjoyed for the first time by many young men who had never found work before and to many older men the purpose of meaningful employment was restored after long lay-offs. Steady work was seen to be such an important element in the maintenance of national morale, that the continuance of full employment became a leading priority of politicians after the war.

There was also a strong demand that the plans for social reconstruction should be laid while the war was still in progress. Sir William Beveridge published his famous report on social security in 1942. He proposed that all citizens should be guaranteed a minimum income and a minimum standard of health, education and housing. More specific plans for the planning of towns were undertaken and in 1944, Parliament passed an Education Act drawn up by R. A. Butler. These plans provided the guide-lines for the development of the Welfare State which has been the main social achievement of Britain since the war. The Second World War therefore had a strong influence on social change and few would dispute that it was change for the better.

FURTHER READING

A. Calder, *The People's War, Britain 1939–45*.
B. Collier, *The Battle of Britain* (Batsford).
Sir A. Harris, *Bomber Offensive* (Oxford).
D. Macintyre, *The Battle of the Atlantic* (Lutterworth).
O. Stewart, *The Story of Air Warfare* (Hamish Hamilton).

9 The Post-War Period

The Nuclear Age

On 16 July 1945 an atomic bomb was successfully exploded in New Mexico, a few months after the war with Germany was over. There was almost unanimous agreement among the delegations at the Potsdam Conference, who were in session to settle the future of Germany, that the weapon should be used against Japan. Atomic bombs were therefore dropped on Hiroshima on 6 August 1945, and on Nagasaki on 8 August; a few days later the Japanese emperor unconditionally surrendered.

The successful development of the weapon had been achieved by British and American scientists and the secrets were not given to the Russians. It soon became clear after the war that the Grand Alliance of Russia, America and Great Britain would not continue after Hitler's defeat. The ideals on which the Russian and American systems of government were based were so diametrically opposed that even agreement on the permanent settlement of Europe was impossible. Stalin's aim was to extend Russian control over Eastern Europe, to extract as much factory machinery from Germany as possible and to keep large armies in existence. His uncompromising attitude arose partly from his fear of the military superiority which America enjoyed with the possession of a nuclear weapon.

Russia soon developed her own nuclear capability, and by 1953 both Russia and America had developed hydrogen bombs, which were so powerful that one was capable of destroying a city the size of London. Meanwhile both sides were developing missiles capable of carrying nuclear warheads from one continent to another. By the end of the 1950s, each was capable of destroying the other completely with its armoury of nuclear weapons in one savage attack. The object of the adversaries then became to survive such a first strike onslaught sufficiently to deliver a similarly devastating retaliatory reply. This was called the second strike potential.

It was not that either side envisaged the use of these weapons. They were developed to dissuade any enemy from attacking them unawares because the enemy felt that they had something to gain. They were kept as a deterrent and an enemy would only be deterred if he knew that the first strike could never win a war. The aim in the 1960s was therefore to develop early warning systems, anti-missile missiles, deep underground systems of delivery with the missiles kept in concrete silos below ground and underwater delivery from Polaris submarines lying on the ocean bed.

The balance of terror maintained between the East represented by the Russian bloc and the West represented by America and her Western allies is called the Cold War. There has been all the rivalry, hostility, preparation and forming of alliances since the war to lead to open war in former circumstances. It is merely the possession of nuclear weapons by both sides since 1949 and the realisation that the use of such weapons could not bring a victory in the accepted sense, that has led them to avoid direct confrontations between their armies.

Although Britain shared in the original development of the atomic bomb, she did not develop weapons as quickly as the two super powers. An atomic bomb was exploded in 1952 and steps were taken to produce hydrogen bombs in 1955, but it soon became clear that Britain could not afford to develop the sophisticated delivery systems. By 1960, Britain was dependent on American technology for the supply of Skybolt missiles and when the Americans cancelled their Skybolt project in 1962, the British government were offered Polaris missiles and technical data relating to the nuclear submarines from which they would be fired. The small number of Polaris submarines that has since been built hardly constitutes an independent nuclear deterrent. It is merely a minor part of the Western defence system.

Post-war involvement

Since the end of the Second World War, Britain has had the commitments of a major world power, without having the resources. An army of occupation had to be maintained in the British zone of Germany (and Austria until 1955),

63 The modern British soldier. He is armed with an automatic weapon and is trained for service anywhere. This soldier was serving in Malaya in 1953 and is dressed for a jungle patrol.

which became a contribution to general European defence. Britain had to bear the burden of withstanding the advance of communism in 1945 by helping the royalist government in Greece against the communist guerillas until President Truman announced that America would aid any country threatened by communism. The Americans also offered all European countries, including Russia, aid in reconstructing their battered lands in the belief that increasing prosperity in itself would halt communist advance. This Marshall Aid began to arrive in 1948, but was refused by Russia on behalf of the whole Eastern bloc, which by this time was divided from Western Europe by a clear frontier called the Iron Curtain. In 1949 most non-neutral Western European countries joined United States and Canada in the North Atlantic Treaty Organisation (NATO) for the common defence of Europe. All participating powers had to contribute forces to be controlled by the Supreme Headquarters of Allied Powers in Europe (SHAPE).

Britain still had a difficult mandate in Palestine after the war. The Jews, who had suffered so severely from persecution at the hands of the Nazis, were flocking towards Palestine as their new national home, while Britain, as the mandatory authority, felt compelled to confine the entry to a yearly quota for the sake of the existing Arab population. The British army there had to deal with a Jewish opposition movement which subjected them to acts of sabotage and even to acts of terrorism. The task was so thankless that the decision was taken to withdraw all British forces by May 1948 and leave the solution of the problem to the United Nations.

Britain also had a peace-keeping function in the Middle East and Far East. As far as western defence was concerned, Britain bore a heavy burden in the Arab states of the Middle East, where she had traditional oil interests and staging bases on the route to the East Indies. Britain's most controversial intervention in the post-war period was in defence of the international ownership of the Suez Canal which was nationalised by Colonel Nasser, president of Egypt, in 1956. Although the capture of the canal was undertaken jointly with the French

64 The war in Korea 1950–53. British troops are seen marching towards the front line to relieve American forces, who bore the brunt of the North Korean attack at first. It was a United Nations Army that fought to drive back the Communist incursion into South Korea.

65 Left: A Jungle patrol. The search for Communist terrorists in Malaya took troops into the most remote parts of the territory. Casualties were carried out by helicopter, but there was often a long and difficult journey to a suitable clearing.

66 Right: Air Rescue from Malaya. Once a clearing had been found or made, the helicopters could land to bring supplies and evacuate casualties.

67 Below: Belfast 1971. The British Army had the difficult task of maintaining order in Ulster in the face of growing IRA activity. August 10, 1971 was a day of rioting after 300 IRA suspects had been arrested. Protestant families evacuated their homes in the Catholic Ardoyne area and set them on fire to prevent the Catholics from taking possession. The vizors on the soldiers helmets are protection from stones.

and the exploit was justified as an attempt to keep the armies of Israel and Egypt apart, the Americans expressed their disapproval through the United Nations. Within a short time the Anglo-French army withdrew. Despite this, the kings and sheikhs of the Persian Gulf still retained their traditional bonds with Great Britain, and Britain maintained her bases in Cyprus and her forces at Bahrein. The garrison at Aden was withdrawn in 1967, and there are many who would like to see Britain evacuate all the bases east of Suez on the grounds of expense.

In the Far East, Britain had the task of withstanding communist and nationalist movements in her colonies especially in Malaya until the Chinese communist guerillas withdrew in 1960 and in North Borneo where the Indonesian government resisted the creation of the Federation of Malaysia between 1963 and 1965. Britain contributed forces to the United Nations army fighting the North Koreans and later the Chinese in the Korean War 1950–53, and in 1954 she joined the South East Asia Treaty Organisation (SEATO), a pact which was not quite the Far Eastern equivalent of NATO as its members, which included the United States, did not surrender their forces to a common alliance command. They merely agreed to consult on matters of common interest.

Britain had some difficult tasks of decolonisation in her other colonies. In Cyprus it has proved impossible to divide responsibility for government between the Turks and the Greeks in an acceptable way. Between 1955 and 1960 an army was tied down there by the need to stop EOKA, a Greek terrorist organisation, seizing control of the island. Another difficult military problem was presented by the Mau Mau in Kenya between 1952 and 1960. The grievance of these Kikuyu tribesmen was concerned with the control of land on the White Highlands, but their campaign took the form of acts of terrorism against the white settlers.

The work that the army had to undertake in Malaya, Kenya, Cyprus and North Borneo was more like police work than formal war. In each case the enemy was small in number, elusive and able to command the support of the local people by the threat of reprisals, if not by genuine sympathy. The wars in the Far East

68 Defoliants. The United States Air Force spraying agriculture defoliants on dense jungle growth in Vietnam in 1966. Missions of this kind designed to destroy vegetation only and were harmless to humans, animals, soil and water.

demanded great skill in jungle warfare in the patrol work and great patience and diplomacy in the task of gaining the confidence of the local people. In each case, time and the systematic harrying of the military elements eventually led to a pacification of the country as the prelude to the granting of independence. Britain now has very few colonies left and these usually have some very special relationship with Britain like Gibraltar or Hong Kong. There is a growing demand for the elimination of the British commitments in the Indian Ocean on the grounds of expense, but there is enough residual common feeling between Britain, Australia and New Zealand for some kind of presence to be maintained in the Far East.

Chemical and Biological Warfare

Until the presence century disease was as likely to cause death in armies through natural causes as was enemy action through the use of weapons. In the present century much research has gone into studying the implications of the artificial spread of disease, not necessarily with a view to its use, but as a safeguard. Germs have not been used as an intentional weapon in modern warfare and are unlikely to be used because it is virtually impossible to control their spread.

Much greater interest has been shown in chemical weapons such as gases and sprays. The first Hague Conference in 1899 forbade the use of poison or poisonous weapons, but it did not condemn gas warfare itself. Gas was used by both sides in the First World War without great success, but enough human suffering was caused for it to be condemned by international agreement at Washington in 1925, together with bacteriological or germ warfare. This agreement was recognised by all belligerents in the Second World War.

Although chemical warfare has been eliminated from the field battle, its potential has been studied anew in the modern limited war, where a small number of irregular fighters supplied from abroad can hold down a huge field army of the country pledged to maintain law and order. Britain has faced post-war situations of this kind in Malaya, Cyprus and Kenya without recourse to chemical warfare, but America has experimented with gases and sprays in Vietnam. Gases have been used to flush the Viet Cong from caves and shelters. They have also made extensive use of defoliants to make the trees lose their leaves and to destroy growing crops in remote areas. This was done to deprive the Viet Cong of their natural hide-outs and to make it difficult for them to survive in inaccessible places.

The lesson of these experiments seems to be that restricted chemical warfare cannot win a war that cannot be won by other means and that the effects on the environment are not entirely predictable. The leaves grow again on the trees in the following spring, but there is damage to fruits and stems which may have a more lasting effect. In using the gases, the object is to immobilise the enemy temporarily by making him vomit and by wracking him with pain. This kind of CS gas is used by British troops in riot control. All major countries also have

69 Pacification. Scots Guards are seen putting up a barbed wire protection around a squatters camp at Sungei Liam, Malaya. In this kind of compound, Chinese squatters from the jungle were resettled with police protection. In their jungle homes they had been forced to supply food and information to the terrorists.

supplies of nerve gas which is colourless, odourless and lethal in very small quantities. The danger of embarking on limited chemical warfare is that it may escalate into the unrestricted use of nerve gases which could prove more deadly than any existing weapon and worse, would affect civilians as badly as soldiers.

The British Army

The present size and form of the British Army retains the ingredients of the army that has developed since 1660. It is a fairly small force of about 150,000 long-service volunteers backed by a smaller band of part-timers in the Army Volunteer Reserve. The regular army still has a world-wide function, no longer as the guardian of the Empire which has been virtually dismantled, but as the executant of Britain's treaty obligations and traditional interests. The Volunteer Reserve provides the link with the Territorial Army, which it recently replaced and with the militia, which preceded it. This dependence on a small, highly-trained army is part of the British military tradition, but its effectiveness has been greatly increased by the use of transport aircraft to carry it quickly to any part of the world. Conscription was retained after the war and until 1960 able-bodied men over eighteen were liable for National Service. This was the first time in British history that there was National Service in peace-time, except for a few months in 1939, and it marks a departure from the British military tradition. Although the small regular army developed since 1960 is a return to the tradition of a highly trained professional mobile force, it is no longer the navy which makes such a meagre military provision possible. Naval superiority, which used to be Britain's greatest strength, has disappeared with the growth of the American and Russian navies. Britain now depends on the effectiveness of the nuclear deterrent and on the firmness of the NATO alliance to which many of our military and naval forces are committed. The Warsaw Pact countries on the opposite side of the Iron Curtain have overwhelming military superiority in troops and conventional weapons, and it is only by the use of nuclear weapons that their advance could be halted.

FURTHER READING

C. Barnett, *Britain and her Army* (Allen Lane, The Penguin Press).

S. E. Ellacott, *Rockets* (Methuen).

S. Rose (ed.), *Chemical and Biological Warfare* (Harrap).

Index

The figures in **bold** type refer to the page numbers of the illustrations.